Life and Mission of
Maulana Mohammad Ilyas

Syed Abul Hasan Ali Nadwi

Translated from Urdu by
Mohammad Asif Kidwai

NADWI PRESS

NADWI PRESS

Nadwi Press Edition

Find our titles on your favourite online bookstore using the keyword 'Nadwi Press'

Originally Published by AIRP, Lucknow (India)
Reprinted by Nadwi Press in 2025

Translation of the Qur'ān

It should be perfectly clear that the Qur'ān is only authentic in its original language, Arabic. Since perfect translation of the Qur'ān is impossible, we have used the translation of the meaning of the Qur'ān throughout the book, as the result is only a crude meaning of the Arabic text.

Qur'ānic verses appear in speech marks proceeded by a reference to the Surah and verse number. Sayings (Hadith) of Prophet Muhammad (saw) appear in inverted commas along with reference to the Hadith Book and its Reporter.

Contents

Forward[1]

In the Name of Allah, the Beneficent, the Merciful

It was more than half a century ago, when I was a student of Darul Uloom, Deoband, that I first heard of Maulana Mohammed Ilyas. I heard that he was teaching the Kalima and Namaz to the Muslims of Mewat, who were Muslims only in name, and establishing Madrassas for the elementary religious education of their children.

Afterwards, I met him a couple of times during my visits to Delhi, but since, at that time, I was not interested in knowing about the Maulana and his work, I remained ignorant of the peerless qualities of his mind and character, his glowing religious fervour and unparalleled struggle, in spite of those meetings.

About forty years before now, however, I came to have some idea, through various sources, of the greatness, of the Maulana and the importance of his *Tabligh* movement. At about the sometime, Maulana Syed Abul Ala Maududi, with whom I had close relations during those days and was very much impressed by his understanding and good judgement, went to Nizamuddin (Delhi) to meet Maulana Mohammed Ilyas and obtain a first-hand knowledge of his work, and, also, undertook a tour of Mewat which was the main centre of Maulana's activities. He, then, published an article in his journal, *Tarjuman-ul- Quran*, giving his impressions of the journey and expressing a high opinion of the *Tabligh* endeavour[2]. I was deeply influenced by that article. My friend, Maulana Syed Abul Hasan Ali Nadwi, the author of the present book, too, was highly

---

[1] Written specially for the English edition.

[2] It appertains to the time when Jama'it-i-Islami had not been found by Maulana Maududi.

impressed, and he was seized with the desire to meet Maulana Mohammed Ilyas and know more about his mission. He, thereupon, visited the Maulana frequently.

In those days, I used to live in Bareilly and kept up a regular correspondence with Maulana Nadwi. From his letters I learnt how he was feeling drawn, more and more, towards Maulana Mohammed Ilyas and the *Tabligh* call he had given. He, also, tried to convince me till a time came when I, too, started going. to Nizamuddin, and, often, both of us went together.

On observing the Maulana from close quarters and accompanying him on *Tabligh* tours and listening to his speeches I arrived at two conclusions.

One was that the Maulana's call was very far- reaching in its effects and based upon solid principles. It was not born out of an impulse, but the product of a deep study of the Quran, the Sunnah and the lives of the holy Companions, and a profound awareness of the nature and spirit of the Faith. The Maulana had devised his course of action after careful thought and there was a definite, well-integrated plan in his mind which contained a full provision for the religious reform and advancement of all sections of the Muslims. He aimed at making belief and conviction and the Islamic way of life and anxiety for Faith common in the Millet.

The other was concerning the personality of the Maulana. The more I knew the Maulana, the more was I impressed by him. Some of my friends endowed with spiritual light and insight were agreed that the existence of the Maulana, in the present times, was a sign of the Power and Authority of God, and a miracle of the sacred Prophet and of the Faith he had brought which had been made manifest as a proof of the permanence and eternity of Islam and with the object of imparting some idea of the religious zeal of the companions and affording a glimpse of the early decades of Islamic glory.

In the Maulana's company, it, also, dawned upon me that however detailed the life-accounts of the godly men may be that are found in the books, they bear no relation to their distinctive personal character and actual moral and spiritual excellence. The natural inclination of the writer or biographer, too, plays a part in the choice of events. During my stay with living masters, I have felt that though no one has displayed a greater regard for authenticity and thoroughness than the writers of the biography of the holy prophet and the compilers of his Traditions, they, after all, have described only what the written word could convey. Still, what has been preserved by the chroniclers and biographers is much more valuable and informative than the accounts that would have reached us simply through recollection and narration. Hence, we find that, today, very little is known about people with regard to whom no such arrangements were made. Led by these considerations, I had begun to note down the more important utterances of the Maulana, and, also, to publish them in Al-Furqan, with his permission and in his own lifetime. Later, a collection of these sayings was brought out in the form of a book, a part of which is included in the present volume as well.

I, also, thought of writing a biography of the Maulana, but could not quite make up my mind as the Maulana was strictly opposed to the association of his call with himself, and towards the ends of his life, he even did not like his name to be mentioned in that connection. Apart from sincerity and self-effacement, the Maulana's care and caution stemmed from important religious considerations. But we must confess our inability to abide wholly by the Maulana's wishes. Sometimes, in the interests of the Movement, it became necessary to describe the spirit of dedication, religious ardour and solicitude for the Faith of its founder and to narrate his personal experiences while explaining its rules and principles or recounting the manifestations of its effect.

In view of all this, it occurred to me, again and again during the Maulana's mortal illness, when my stay was mostly at Nizamuddin, that his biography, including a detailed account of the *Tabligh* movement, should be written. When I discussed it with Maulana Syed Abul Hasan Ali Nadwi who was, also, staying there in those days, I found that he, too, was thinking on the same lines, and had even started preparing notes. Anyhow, on the Maulana's death, it was decided to go ahead with the task.

Almost all the old colleagues and relatives of the Maulana had collected at Nizamuddin at that time and Maulana Nadwi took the opportunity to gather facts from them. The correspondence of the Maulana, also, was made available to him. The Maulana had, perhaps, written the most detailed letters concerning the aims and principles of the Movement to Maulana Nadwi himself. Some other friends, too, sent to him the Maulana's letters which were in their possession and furnished other valuable information when they came to know that he was writing the book. The help and co-operation extended by Sheikhul Hadees Maulana Mohammed Zakaria proved most beneficial.

When the manuscript was ready, it was circulated among the Maulana's trusted colleagues and close relatives for advice, and was, also, read out at different gatherings during the *Tabligh* tour so that nothing was left to be desired by way of accuracy or detail.

Before concluding, I would like to stress that though the author has admirably succeeded in his effort and no one could have done greater justice to the subject, whatever impression the readers who had not come into contact with the Maulana will form about him from these pages will be much short of what he actually was. My own case is that it was only during the Maulana's last illness that I had the good fortune to observe him closely, and I can say without hesitation that every day I felt that he was much greater than what I had imagined the previous day.

About four months before the Maulana's death, a godly man of the highest class had remarked that "now-a-days he (the Maulana) is travelling at the speed of thousands of miles per hour" I could not grasp its significance then, but as I became more aware of the Maulana's inner state, I realised what. journey did he have in mind.

The Maulana, often, said about his Movement that it was a jewel of the golden era (of Islam). About the Maulana himself I can say, without exaggeration, that he was a pearl of the magnificent treasure-house of that time. We read much about the celebrated precursors in the books which seems hard to believe to our materialistic minds, but on seeing those things, with my own eyes, in the Maulana, I gained such satisfaction as could not be possible with the help of a thousand arguments.

In this book, too, readers will find statements regarding the Maulana and his ancestors which may appear incredible in the present-day world of bigotry and shallowness, but the author has fully verified them and included only the facts that came to his knowledge through reliable sources. In fact, most of the incidents. related here concerning the Maulana took place in the author's own presence either in a *Tabligh* journey or during his stay at Nizamuddin.

The book deals more with the call and mission of the Maulana than his life. But it was natural for the main object of the author has been to make the world acquainted with the Maulana's unique endeavour for the revival and preservation of faith.

Mohammed Manzoor Nomani

Lucknow

December 25, 1978

Chapter I: Early days

On the outskirts of Delhi, near the tomb of Khwaja Nizamuddin, there lived, some seventy years ago[1], a godly person in the house on top of the red gate of the historical building called Chaunsath Khamba[2]. His name was Maulana Mohammad Ismail.

The ancestral home of Maulana Mohammad Ismail was in Jhanjhana, in the district of Muzaffarnagar. But when, after the death of his first wife, he married again in the family of Mufti Ilahi Bakhsh Kandhlawi, who belonged to the same ancestry as him, he visited Kandhla frequently and it became a second home to him.

The family of Siddiqui Shaikhs of Jhanjhana and Kandhla had known, for generations, for piety and learning, and was held in high esteem in the neighbourhood. The lines of descent of Maulana Mohammad Ismail and Mufti Ilahi Bakhsh became one, six generations upwards, with Molvi Mohammad Sharif. The lineage runs as follows: Maulana Mohammad Ismail, son of Ghulam Husain, son of Hakim Karim Bakhsh, son of Hakim Ghulam Mohiuddin, son of Molvi Mohammad Sajid, son of Molvi Mohammad Faiz, son of Molvi Mohammad Sharif, son of Molvi Mohammad Ashraf , son of Sheikh Jamal Mohammad Shah, son of Sheikh Baban Shah, son of Sheikh Bahauddin Shah, son of Molvi Mohammad Sheikh, son of Sheikh Mohammad Fazil, son of Es- Sheikh Qutub shah.

Mufti Ilahi Bakhsh was among the most outstanding pupils of Shah Abdul Aziz. Besides being a distinguished teacher, author and legist, he was, also, a Unani physician of a high order, and

---

[1] It was written 35 years ago.

[2] Meaning a building with 64 pillars.

possessed a thorough knowledge of both the rational and traditional sciences. He had a great command over Arabic, Persian and Urdu poetry as well, as is borne out by his commentary of Banat su'ad in which he has translated every line of Hazrat K'ab into Arabic, Persian and Urdu verse. He left behind about 40 books in Arabic and Persian of which Shiyamul Habib and Mathnawi Maulana Rum Ka Takmila[1] are more famous.

Mufti Ilahi Bakhsh had taken *ba'it*[2] at the hand of Shah Abdul Aziz. A glowing proof of his sincerity and selflessness was that though he was a renowned spiritual mentor himself, on the death of Shah Abdul Aziz, he felt no hesitation in taking bait at the hand of the latter's young deputy, Syed Ahmad Shaheed, who was about 28 years his junior in age, and in seeking guidance from him.

Mufti Sahib was born in 1748, and died in 1831, at the age of 83 years. All his sons and grandsons were men of learning and position. Scholarship and religiousness have been the characteristics of this family. Molvi Abul Hasan's Mathnawi, Gulzar-i-Ibrahim, which forms a part of his well-known work, Bahr-i-Haqiqat, is a poem of rare spiritual feeling. Till recently, it was very popular. His son, Molvi Nurul Hasan, and all the four grandsons, Molvi Ziaul Hasan, Molvi Akbar, Molvi Sulaiman and Hakim Molvi

---

[1] The *Mathnawi* is a sort of long poem in which the couplets rhyme regularly. The Mathnawi of Jalaluddin Rumi. Known popularly as Mathnawi Maulana Rum. is a work of everlasting value and a priceless gem of Persian and Islamic literature. Mufti Ilahi Bakhsh wrote its Takmila, meaning addition to a book with a view to bring it to completion. It is considered a masterpiece.

[2] Meaning a 'vow' or 'pledge'. In Islamic parlance, it denotes a solemn pledge of loyalty and devotion given to a leader by his followers.

Ibrahim, attained to fame as worthy representatives of their celebrated ancestors.

Mufti Saheb's nephew, Maulana Muzaffar Hussain, who was a most favourite pupil of Shah Is'haq and a deputy of Shah Mohammad Yaqub, and had, also, been favoured with the company of Syed Ahmad Shaheed, was a very pious and godly person. He never touched anything that was of doubtful purity in the eyes of the Shariat. Incidents of his humility and prayerfulness are still fresh in the memory of the people of the neighbouring areas and serve as a reminder to the glorious days of the earliest decades of Islam.

The maternal granddaughter of Maulana Muzaffar Husain was married to Maulana Mohammad Ismail. It was his second marriage, which was solemnised on October 30, 1868.

Maulana Mohammad Ismail was the tutor of the children of Mirza Ilahi Bakhsh, who was related to Bahadur Shah Zafar, the last of the Mughal Emperors. He lived, as we have seen, in the house, on top of the red gate of Chaunsath Khamba. Close to it, was a small mosque with a tin shed in front which used to serve as the parlour of Mirza Ilahi Bakhsh, and, owing to it, it was called Bangle Wali Masjid.[1]

The Maulana was spending his days in obscurity and even Mirza Ilahi Bakhsh had no idea of his high station till he had a personal experience of how the Maulana's prayers were granted by God.

Worship, Zikr (repeating the Names, Praises and Attributes of the Lord), attending to the needs of the travellers and teaching

[1] Meaning the mosque with a shed.

the Quran and giving instruction. in the faith were his sole occupation in life. He used to take down the load from the heads of the thirsty labourers who passed that way, place it on the ground, draw water from the well and give it to them to drink, and then, offer two *Rak'ats*[1] of Namaz, expressing gratitude to the Lord that He had given him the opportunity to serve His bondmen, though he did not deserve it. He had attained the state of *Ihsan.*[2]

Once, as he requested Maulana Rasheed Ahmad Gangohi to teach him Sulook[3], the latter remarked, "You don't need it. You have already attained the objective that is to be reached through this method. It is like a person who has read the Quran saying that he should, also, read the elementary textbook of Arabic because he had not begun with it."

The Maulana was very fond of the recitation of the Quran. An old wish of his was that he went on grazing the goats and reciting the Quran. He was very particular about some member of his family keeping vigil in the night. His second son, Maulana Yahya, used to study till midnight and, then the Maulana himself got up and Maulana Yahya went to bed and for the last part of the night, he woke up his eldest son, Maulana Mohammad.

The Maulana never bores a grudge against anyone. His detachment with the world was so complete that it had made him attached to everybody All the persons who came into contact with him were impressed by his piety, sincerity and selflessness. Leaders

---

[1] The Namaz consists of many cyclic parts which are known as *Rak'ats.*

[2] Meaning to worship as if God was seeing the bondsman and the bonds. man was seeing Him.

[3] Literally, the 'path' or 'way'. In the special terminology of *Tasawwuf* (Islamic Mysticism), it denoteric or mystical path.

of the different warring groups of Delhi held him in the highest esteem, and put an equal trust in him, though they disliked each other so much that none of them was willing to offer Namaz behind the other.

The link with Mewat, too, was established in his lifetime. It is related that, once, he went out in the hope of finding a Muslim whom he could bring to the mosque and offer Namaz with him. On meeting some Muslim labourers, he enquired from them where they were going. "We are going in search of work", they replied. "How much do you expect to earn?" asked the Maulana. The labourers, thereupon, told him about the daily wages they, generally, received. "If you get the same here," the Maulana asked, "What is the use of going else where?" The labourers agreed and the Maulana took them to the mosque and began to teach them Namaz and the Quran. He would pay them their wages every day and keep them engaged in their lessons. In a few days, they developed the habit of offering up Namaz. Such was the beginning of the Madrassa[1] of Bangle Wali Masjid, and these labourers were its first scholars. After it, about ten Mewati students always remained in the Madrassa and their meals used to come from the house of Mirza Ilahi Bakhsh.

Maulana Mohammad Ismail died on 26th February 1898 in Khajoor Wali Masjid[2] at the *Tiraha*[3] of Bahram in Delhi. The number of mourners, at his funeral, was so large that though long bamboo poles had been tied to the either sat beside of the bier to enable them to lend a shoulder to it, many people did not get a chance during the entire route of three- and-a-half miles from Delhi to Nizamuddin.

---

[1] A seminary. It, generally, denotes a school for the diffusion of Islamic learning.

[2] Meaning the mosque with date-palms.

[3] An area bounded by three streets.

Muslims belonging to various sects and schools of thought, who never got together joined the procession. The Maulana's second son, Maulana Mohammad Yahya, narrates that "my elder brother, Maulana Mohammad, was a very soft-hearted person and had a most obliging nature. Fearing that he might invite someone to lead the funeral service behind which people of another sect or group refused to offer the prayer, and, thus, an unpleasant situation arose, I stepped forward and said that I would lead the service. Everyone, then, offered up the prayers peacefully and there was no dissent or commotion."

Owing to the vast concourse of men, the funeral service had to be held a number of times and the burial was delayed. During it, a venerable person and another man known for his spirituality had a vision that Maulana Mohammad Ismail was saying, "Send me off soon. I am feeling ashamed. The holy Prophet is waiting for me."

The Maulana had three son: Maulana Mohammad from the first wife, and Maulana Mohammad Yahya and Maulana Mohammad Ilyas from the second, who was the maternal granddaughter of Maulana Muzaffar Husain. The Maulana had married her after the death of his first wife.

Maulana Muhammad Ilyas

Maulana Mohammad Ilyas was born in 1885. His childhood was spent in his maternal grandfather's home in Kandhla, and with his father at Nizamuddin. In those days, the Kandhla family was the cradle of godliness and piety so much so that reports of the high religiosity, nightly devotions and *Zikr*[1] and *Tilawat*[2] of its members, both male and female, would seem imaginary and fictitious to the faint-hearted men of our time.

The ladies used to recite the Quran themselves in the *Nafl*[3] prayers as well as listen to its recital in *Tarawih*[4] and other *Nafl* prayers, standing behind the male relatives. The month of Ramzan, in particular, was the springtime for the Quran. It was read for long hours, almost in every home. The limit of absorption was that, sometimes, the ladies forgot to pay attention to Purdah and would not become aware of the coming of outsiders in the house at a time of urgent need.[5]

The Quran with its translation and commentary in Urdu, and Mazaahir-i-Haq, Mashariq-ul-Anwaar, and Hisn-i-Haseen formed the limit of the education of the ladies. Deeds and accomplishments of the families of Syed Ahmad Shaheed and Shah Abdul Aziz were the most popular themes of conversation, and facts regarding these illustrious men of God were on everybody's lips. Instead of the stories of kings and fairies, ladies of the household related these events to the children.

The Maulana's maternal grandmother, Amtus Salam, who was the daughter of Maulana Muzaffar Husain and was known in the family as Ammi Bi, was a very pious lady About her Namaz, the

---

[1] Repeating the Names. Praises and Attributes of God.

[2] Recitation of The Quran.

[3] Meaning non-obligatory.

[4] Special prayers offered in the month of Ramzan at night.

[5] Once. after narrating some incidents of a like nature, Maulana Mohammad Ilyas remarked that "these were the laps in which I was brought up. Where, in the world, are such laps to be found today?"

Maulana, once, observed that "I saw the likeness of Ammi Bi's Namaz in the Namaz of Maulana Gangohi."

During the last phase of life, Ammi Bi's state was that she never asked for food and ate only when someone placed it before her. It was a large family and there was always so much to do. If the thought of having her meal did not occur to her in the midst of domestic chores, she simply went hungry. Once, someone said to her, "You are so old and weak. How do you manage to go without food?" "I draw sustenance from my *Tasbihat*[1], was her reply.

The mother of Maulana Mohammad Ilyas, Bi Safia, had learnt the Quran by heart and attained great distinction in it. It was a regular practice with her to recite the whole of the Quran and additional ten *Paras*[2] every day during Ramzan. She, thus, completed forty recitals of the Quran in that month and was so fluent in it that her household duties did not suffer on account of it. She, generally, kept herself engaged in some work while doing the recitation. Apart from the month of Ramzan, her daily routine of worship included: Durood Sharif, 5,000 times; *Ism- i- Zaat Allah*, 5,000 times; *Bismillah ar-Rahman, ar- Rahim*, 1,000 times; *Yaa- Mughnee- u*, 1,100 times; *La illaaha illallaah*, 1,200 times; *Ya Haiyyu, Yaqaiyum*, 200 times; *Hasbiallaah wa ni'mul Vakil*, 500 times; *Subhan Allah*, 200 times; *Al-Hamdu lillaah*, 200 times; *La ilaaha illallaah*, 200 times; *Allah- o- Akbar*, 200 times; *Istighfar*, 500 times; *Ofwwizu amree illallaah*, 100, times; *Hasbunallaah wa ni'mul Vakil*, 1000 times; *Rabb- i- in- ni maghloobun fantasir*, 1,000 times; *Rabb- i- inni masanni- az- zurru wa anta ar- hamur rahimeen*, 100 times; *Laa ilaaha illa you subhanaka in- ni kuntu minaz-*

---

[1] Plural of *Tasbih* and meaning a rosary or string of beads on which prayers are counted. It. also. denotes the acts of praising the Lord.

[2] The Quran is divided into 30 parts, popularly called paras or Si-Paras.

zalimeen, 100 times. In addition, she recited a Manzil[1] of the Quran every day.

Like all other children in the family, the maulana began his education in the *maktab*[2], and, according to the family tradition, learnt the Quran by heart. The learning of the Quran was so common in the family, that in the one- and-a-half row of worshippers in the family mosque, there was not a single non-Hafiz[3] except the *Muezzin*[4].

Maulana Mohammad Ilyas was Ammi Bi's favourite child. She used to say to him. "Ilyas, I feel the aroma of the holy Companions in you." Sometimes, placing her hand on his back, she would say, "How is it that I see figures resembling the holy Companions moving along with you?

From his childhood, there was present in Maulana Mohammad Ilyas a touch of the religious ardour and fervent feeling of the blessed Companions, which had led Sheikhul Hind Maulana Mahmood Hasan to remark that "when I see Mohammad Ilyas, I am reminded of the holy Companions."

Eagerness and enthusiasm for faith were ingrained in his nature. Even in his early days, he, sometimes, did things which were much above the common level of the children. Riazul Islam Kandhlawi, a class fellow of his in the Maktab, says that "when we were reading in Maktab he i.e., Maulana Mohammad Ilyas, once,

---

[1] The Quran is divided into seven Manzils, each beginning with a particular Sura.

[2] A primary school of traditional design:

[3] One who has done the whole Quran by heart is called Hafiz.

[4] The public orier to prayers among the Muslims.

came with a stick and said, "Come, Riazul Islam, let us do *Jehad*[1] against those who do not offer up Namaz'.'

Stay at Gangoh

In 1893, his elder brother, Mohammad Yahya, went to live at Gangoh with Maulana Rasheed Ahmad Gangohi. Maulana Mohammad Ilyas used to live with his father at Nizamuddin, and, sometimes, with his maternal grand-father's family at Kandhla. At Nizamuddin, his education was being neglected owing to the over-fondness of his father and his own excessive occupation with prayers. Maulana Yahya, thus, requested his father that as he education of Mohammad Ilyas was suffering, he might be allowed to take him to Gangoh. The father agreed and Maulana Mohammad Ilyas came to Gangoh in 1896 or early 1897 where Mohammad Yahya began to teach him regularly.

Gangoh, in those days, was the seat of Sufi-saints and savants, the benefit of whose company was constantly available Maulana Mohammad Ilyas. A greater part of his impressionable age was spent there. When he went to live at Gangoh, he was 10 or 11 years old, and at the time of Maulana Rasheed Ahmed Gangohi's death, in 1905, he was a young man of about 20. Thus, he stayed with Maulana Gangohi for about 9 years.

Maulana Mohammad Yahya was an ideal teacher and benefactor Ile wanted his brother to derive the utmost advantage from the society of those illustrious men. Maulana Mohammad Ilyas used to tell that when the Ulema who had been the favourite pupils or disciples of Maulana Gangohi came to Gangoh, his brother would,

---

[1] Meaning a holy war.

often, stop the lessons and say that his education, then, lay in sitting with them and listening to their conversation.

Usually, Maulana Gangohi did not take bait from children and students. It was only when they had completed their education that he allowed them to take the pledge. But owing to the exceptional merit of Maulana Mohammad Ilyas, he, at his request, permitted him to do the bait at his hand.

Maulana Mohammad Ilyas had been born with a loving heart. Such a strong attachment did he develop for Maulana Gangohi that he felt no peace without him. He would, often, get up in the night, go and see the Maulana's face, and return to his bed. Maulana Gangohi, too, had a great affection for him. Once, Maulana Mohammad Ilyas told his brother, Maulana Mohammad Yahya, that if the maulana consented, he would sit near him while studying. As Maulana Mohammad Yahya conveyed the request to Maulana Gangohi, he remarked, "There is no harm in it. My privacy will not be disturbed by the presence of Ilyas, nor will it affect the peace of my mind."

At the time of *Zikr*, Maulana Mohammad Ilyas used to feel a sort of load on his heart. When he mentioned it to Maulana Gangohi, the Maulana shuddered. he said that "Maulana Mohammad Qasim had complained of a similar feeling to Haji Imdadullah, upon which Haji Saheb had observed that God was going to take some special service from him."

Maulana Mohammad Yahya's method of teaching was original. He did not begin with teaching books, in the primary stage, but dictated rules of grammar to the pupils, and then, gave them two-letter or three-letter words to conjugate and inflect. Emphasis was laid on literature from the beginning. He started with Shah

Waliullah's *chahl Hadees*[1] and the *Sipara* of *'Aam* and said that as a Muslim child knew the *Sipara* by heart, he needed not learn the words, but only their meanings. He would, however, add that the words of Hadees[2] and the Quran possessed a propitiousness of their own.

The Maulana's main concern was the development of the mental faculties of the pupils. He did not even care whether a book was completed or not. Generally, he gave a book, without notes and explanations, to the students to read unaided, and when he was satisfied that he could read and explain a sufficient number of its pages properly, he gave him another book. It went a long way to develop the virtue of self-confidence in his pupils.

Maulana Mohammad Ilyas's health had never been good. At Gangoh, it deteriorated further, and he began to have attacks of severe headache after which he could not bend his head even to the extent of performing the *Sajda*[3] on a pillow for months. Maulana Gangohi's son, Hakim Masud Ahmad, who was his physician, had a peculiar method of treatment. In certain diseases, he forbade the use of water for a long time, which was unbearable to most of the patients. But with the strength of mind that was so characteristic of him, Maulana Mohammad Ilyas abided strictly by the advice of his physician and abstained from drinking water for full seven years, and, during the next five years, he drank it only sparingly.

---

[1] Meaning a compilation of Forty Traditions. Different scholars have brought out collections of forty different Traditions, one such collection is, also, by Shah Waliullah which contains short and simple sayings of the Prophet.

[2] Meaning the Traditions of the Prophet.

[3] Act of prostration with the forehead touching the ground.

There was little hope that he would be able to resume his education after the discontinuation owing to illness. He was very keen to take it up again, but his well-wishers would not allow. Would not allow. One day, as Maulana Mohammad Yahya said to him what he would, in any case, do by studying, he retorted, "What will I do by living?" Ultimately, he succeeded in resuming his studies.

The death of Maulana Gangohi occurred in 1905. Maulana Mohammad Ilyas, who was at his bedside during the dying moments and reciting the *Sura of Ya-Sin*, was so deeply affected by it that he used, often, to say, "Two shocks have been most painful to me. One was of the death of my father, and the other, of the death of Maulana Rasheed Ahmad Gangohi."

In 1908, Maulana Mohammad Ilyas went to Deoband, where he studied Tirmizi and Sahih Bukhari from Maulana Mahmood Hasan. There, latter advised him to approach Maulana Khalil Ahmad Saharanpuri for spiritual guidance and instruction, since his mentor, Maulana Rasheed Ahmad Gangohi, was no more, and, thus, he completed the various stages of Sulook under Maulana Saharanpuri's supervision.

Absorption in prayers

During his stay at Gangoh, after the death of Maulana, Maulana Mohammad Ilyas generally remained silent and spent of his time in meditation. Says Maulana Mohammad Zakaria, "We read elementary Persian from him in those days. His practice, then, was that he sat cross-legged, and in utter silence, on a coarse mat behind the tomb of Shah Abdul Quddus. We presented ourselves for the lesson, opened the book, and placed it before him, indicating with the finger where we were to begin from on that day. We would read aloud and translate the Persian verses. When we made a mistake, he would shut the book with a movement of the finger, and the lesson came to an end. It meant that we were to go back, prepare the lesson thoroughly, and then, come again He used to offer *Nafl* prayers much and often at that time. From Maghrib[1] till a little before *Isha*[2], he devoted himself exclusively to *Nawafil*[3] His age, then, was between 20 and 25 years."

Ardour and eagerness

Ardour and eagerness, without which no real success is possible in any field, were deeply rooted in him. It was by sheer determination and earnestness that he accomplished what he did in spite of persistent ill health.

One day, during his last illness, Maulana Mohammad Ilyas related that "Once I was so ill and feeling so weak that I could not go down the stairs. All of a sudden, I heard that Maulana Saharanpuri had come to Delhi and was so excited that I left for Delhi immediately on foot and forgot all about my illness and exhaustion. It was in the way that I remembered I was sick."

Contact with other spiritual mentors.

Regular contact with other spiritual mentors and disciples of Maulana Gangohi was maintained during those days. About Shah Abdur Rahim Raipuri and Maulana Ashraf Ali Thanwi, he used to say

---

[1] The evening prayer offered immediately after sunset.

[2] The prayer of the first watch of the night.

[3] Plural of Nafl.

that they abided in his heart. They, too, had a great regard and affection for him owing to his extraordinary qualities.

Spirit of Jehad

Together with *Zikr*, *Ashghaal*[1], *Nawafil* and *Ibadaat*[2], Maulana Mohammad Ilyas was, also, infused with the spirit of *Jehad*.[3] Throughout his life, he was never without it, and had, in fact, taken the pledge of *Jehad* at the hand of Maulana Mahmood Hasan for that very reason.

Estimation in the eyes of elders

From his early days, he was held in the highest esteem by the elders of the family as well as the spiritual leaders of the day. Maulana Mohammad Yahya was like a father to him, yet the former's attitude towards his younger brother was like that of the sacred prophet towards Hazrat Usman.

Indifferent health prevented him from taking part in duties involving physical labour. He concentrated wholly on his studies, and on Zikr, and other forms of worship. Maulana Mohammad Yahya, on the contrary, was a very industrious person. He owned a bookshop, which he managed with great care. It was not only his source of livelihood, but of his brothers as well. One day, the manager of the shop said that Maulana Mohammad Ilyas did not take any interest in the business, which was not good for he, too,

---

[1] Denoting spiritual exercises and exertions.

[2] Plural of Ibadat meaning worship.

[3] To strive to the utmost, even to the extent of laying down one's life, in the path of God.

benefited from it. When Maulana Mohammad Yahya heard of it, he was very angry and remarked that "a Tradition has it that the sustenance that reaches you and the help you receive from the Lord is due to the blessedness of the weaker ones among you." I believe that I am receiving my sustenance owing to the good fortune of this child. Nothing should be said to him in future. If there is anything to say, it should be said to me."

Sometimes, Maulana Mohammad Ilyas was asked to lead the service in the presence of renowned theologians and spiritual leaders. Once Shah Abdur Rahim Raipuri, Maulana Khalil Ahmad Saharanpuri and Maulana Ashraf Ali Thanwi happened to be in Kandhla. When the time for Namaz came and Maulana Mohammad Ilyas was asked to lead it, a senior member of the family, Molvi Badrul Hasan, humorously remarked that "such a small engine has been fastened to so many big carriages." "It depends on the power (not the size) of the engine", replied one of them.

Career as a teacher in Mazaahiri Uloom

In 1910, a large number of men, including most of the senior teachers of the Madrassa of Mazahirul Uloom, left for the Haj from Saharanpur. It necessitated the recruitment of new teachers for the Madrassa, Maulana Mohammad Ilyas being one of them. He was given the secondary books to teach. On the return of the senior teachers from the Pilgrimage, all the new entrants were relieved of their duties, but the services of Maulana Mohammad Ilyas were retained.

At Mazaahirul Uloom, the Maulana had to teach some books which he had not read himself as, in Maulana Mohammad Yahya's scheme of instruction, it was not customary to complete the books, and Maulana Mohammad Ilyas, further, had to miss some secondary books owing to ill-health. During his teaching days, he tried hard to make up for the deficiency and prepared his lectures carefully. For instance, for teaching *Kinzul Daqa'iq.* He studied *Bahr- ur-Ra'iq, Shaami and Hadya*, and consulted even Hisami's notes and comments when he taught Nurul Anwaar.

Marriage

The Maulana married the daughter of his maternal uncle, Maulana Rauful Hasan, on Friday, October 17, 1912. The Nikah was performed by Maulana Mohammad, and Maulana Khalil Ahmad Saharanpuri, Shah Abdur Rahim Raipuri and Maulana Ashraf ali Thanwi, all the three of them, attended the ceremony. Maulana Thanwi's celebrated sermon, *Fuwayid-us-Suhbat*, which has subsequently been published times without number, was delivered on that occasion.

First Haj

In 1915, Maulana Khalil Ahmad Saharanpuri and Maulana Mahmood Hasan, decided to go on the Hajj Pilgrimage. When Maulana Mohammad Ilyas came to know of it, he was strongly seized with the desire to perform the Haj. He felt that it would become dark and gloomy in India with their departure, and he would not be able to live in Saharanpur any more. But there was the question of permission. As his sister, the wife of Maulvi Ikramul Hasan, saw his distress, she offered her ornaments to meet the expenses of the Pilgrimage. Contrary to expectation, the Maulana's mother gave her consent, after which Maulana Mohammad Yahya, also, agreed. The Maulana, then, wrote to Maulana Khalil Ahmad Saharanpuri asking for his permission, and explained that as far as the wherewithal for the journey was concerned, three courses were open to him.

He could take his sister's ornaments or borrow the amount or accept the offers of money made by certain relatives. Maulana Khalil Ahmad Saharanpuri preferred the third course.

Maulana Mohammad Ilyas was fortunate enough to travel by the same boat as Maulana Khalil Ahmad Saharanpuri. He sailed in August 1914, and returned in February 1915, to resume the teaching at the Madrassa.

Death of Maulana Muhammad Yahya

The death of Maulana Mohammad Yahya, on Wednesday, the 9th of August 1915, was an extremely sad and frustrating event for the Maulana. In addition to being a most affectionate brother, he was, also, his teacher and benefactor. He could not get over the shock till the end of his days. He used to get lost in thought and a peculiar kind of abstraction took possession of him when he talked about his brother.

Chapter II: Stay at Nizamuddin

Two years after the death of Maulana Mohammad Yahya, the eldest brother of Maulana Mohammad Ilyas, Maulana Mohammad, also, passed away. He was a man of angelic disposition and an embodiment of affection, piety, and humility. He loved solitude and cared little for worldly comforts. He lived in Bangle Wali Masjid, at Nizamuddin, in the place of his late father. There was a Madrassa in the mosque, which has been founded by Maulana Mohammad Ismail. Only primary education was imparted in it, and, among its pupils were mostly the children from Mewat. It had no regular source of income, and reliance was placed solely upon God for meeting its needs.

Many people of Delhi and Mewat were devoted to Maulana Mohammad and had benefited from his guidance. His face had the radiance of spirituality. He, often, gave the sermon, but in an informal, conversational way. He remained seated during it, and, generally, read out the Traditions on good morals and *Zuhd*[1], and explained their meaning in a simple language.

Once, Maulana Mohammad developed a boil under an eye, which had to be opened seven times. The doctors insisted on administering the anaesthetic, but he refused to take it and lay motionless throughout the operation. The surgeon, afterwards, said that he had not seen the like of it in his life.

Maulana Mohammad spent most of his time in prayer and meditation. During the 16 years before his death, he did not miss the

---

[1] Islamic asceticism.

Tahajjud[1] prayers even once, and breathed his last while performing the Sajda in the Namaz of *Witr*[2].

Maulana Mohammad Ilyas had come to Delhi to look after his sick brother and was staying with him in the Nawab Wali Masjid of Qassab Pura. It was there that Maulana Mohammad died and the burial took place at Nizamuddin. Thousands of men attended the funeral.

After the burial, people urged upon Maulana Mohammad Ilyas to take up residence at Nizamuddin in order to fill the void caused by the death of his father and brother. They, also, promised monthly donations for the Madrassa to which the Maulana agreed subject to certain conditions, which he observed throughout his life.

Maulana Mohammad Ilyas had made it clear that he would come to Nizamuddin and take charge of the Madrassa only if Maulana Khalil Ahmad Saharanpuri approved. Upon it, several persons offered to go to Saharanpur to obtain the permission, but Maulana Mohammad Ilyas checked them saying that it was not the way to do it. He would go himself, unaccompanied by anyone.

The Maulana, thus, went to Saharanpur and explained the whole thing to Maulana Khalil Ahmad. The latter gave his approval, but added that, in the first instance, only a year's leave be taken from Mazaahirul Uloom and if the stay at Nizamuddin proved useful and it was decided to settle down there permanently, he could resign at any time.

But before Maulana Mohammad Ilyas could move to Nizamuddin, he was suddenly taken ill with pleurisy and went to

---

[1] A form of Namaz said during the later part of the night.

[2] A prayer offered at the end of the Namaz of Isha.

Kandhla where his condition worsened. One night his illness took such a grave turn that all hope was lost. The pulse sank and the body became cold, but God had to take some work from him, Unexpectedly, he began to improve, and, in a few days, was able to leave the bed.

On regaining health, Maulana came to Nizamuddin from Kandhla. In those days, there was no habitation in that part of Nizamuddin, and, adjoining the mosque, there was a thick growth of trees and underbrush. Maulana Ihtishamul Hasan who, in his childhood, had come to live, for some time, with Maulana Mohammad Ilyas tells that "I used to go out and stand in the hope of seeing a human face. When anyone appeared, I felt so happy as if someone had given me a precious gift."

A small pucca[1] mosque, a shed, a living apartment, a small settlement of the settlement of the attendants of the tomb to the south of it, and a few Mewati and non-Mewati students that was all that formed the world of the mosque and the Madrassa.

The resources of the Madrassa were so meagre that, sometimes, they had to starve, but the Maulana bore it all with a cheerful heart. Occasionally, he would say, plainly, that there was nothing to eat. Whoever wanted to stay might stay and whoever wanted to go might go and make his arrangement elsewhere. The moral and spiritual training the students were receiving, however, was such that none of them was willing to leave. Often, they would live on wild fruits. The scholars themselves brought wood from the forest to prepare the *chappatis*[2], which they ate with *Chutney*[3]. The

---

[1] Meaning built of brick.

[2] A thin cake of unbeavered dough.

[3] A kind of pickle.

extreme poverty made no impression on the Maulana. What worried him was the prospect of abundance and prosperity which, he was sure, was going to open up, according to the practice of the Lord, after the phase of trial and tribulation.

The outward appearance of the Madrassa held no interest for the Maulana. He was supremely unconcerned! With it. Once, during his absence, some residential quarters were built for its staff through the efforts of Haji Abdur Rahman, an old friend of his and an ex-student of the Madrassa, which made the Maulana so angry that he did not speak to him for a long time. The Maulana remarked that the real thing was education, and, referring to a certain Madrassa, said that its building had become pucca, but the standard of education had gone down.

Once a prominent of Delhi begged the Maulana to supplicate to the Lord for him in a very important matter and presented him a purse. The Maulana agreed to pray on his behalf but declined to accept the money. Haji Abdur Rahman, however, took it in view of the chronic financial difficulties of the Madrassa, but the Maulana had no peace until he had it returned. He used to impress upon Haji Abdur Rahman that the work of faith was not carried out with money, otherwise much wealth would have been granted to the holy Prophet.

Worshipfulness

Maulana Mohammad Ilyas, exclusively, kept himself occupied with prayers and other spiritual exertions in those days. He had inherited the inclination for it from his ancestors, which blossomed up during the stay at Nizamuddin. He sought solitude and carried out vigorous exercises for the purification of the soul.

According to Haji Abdur Rahman, the Maulana remained in seclusion for long hours at the gate of Arab Sara which was the favourite place of worship of Hazrat Nizamuddin Auliya, and was situated to Stay at Nizamuddin the north of Humayun's tomb, near the mausoleum of Abdur Rahim Khan Khana and the grave of Syed Nur Mohammad Badayuni, the spiritual mentor of Mirza Mazhar Jan-i- Janan. Usually, his mid-day meal was sent there while the evening meal he took at home. He offered the five daily prayers in congregation. Haji Abdur Rahman and his fellow-students used to go to the gate to form the congregation, and for their lessons, they, sometimes, went there, and sometimes, the Maulana himself came to Chukkar Wali Masjid.

The maulana performed the *Wuzu* and offered two *Rak'ats* of Namaz before commencing the lesson of the Traditions, and remarked that the claim of the Traditions was even greater. He did not talk to anyone, however important, while teaching the Traditions, nor ever complained if the meal came late from Nizamuddin, nor found fault with food.

Interest in teaching

The Maulana took a keen interest in his pupils and personally taught all the subjects, elementary as well as advanced. Sometimes, he had as many as eighty students directly under his instruction and took the class of Mustadrak-i-Haakim before *Fajr*[1].

The main emphasis in his method of teaching was on the application of mind. He wanted the students to come thoroughly prepared. The Maulana did not follow the general syllabus of the

[1] The early morning prayer offered between dawn and sunrise.

Madrassas in the selection of books and many books that were not prescribed in the other Madrassas were taught at Nizamuddin. He thought of new ways to stimulate the students and develop the faculties of imagination and understanding in them.

Chapter III:
Beginning of the movement of religious reform in Mewat

The area to the south of Delhi where the Meos have been settled from the olden days is called Mewat. Presently, it includes the Gurgaon district of the Punjab, the native states of Alwar and Bharatpur and the district of Mathura of the United Provinces. Like all other regions, its boundaries, too, have been changing from time to time and the dimensions of the old Mewat must have been different from what they are now.

The English historians hold that the Meos do not come from the Aryan stock but are related to the non-Aryan races of ancient India. Their history, thus, dates far back than that of the Rajput Families of Aryan blood. According to them, the *Khanzadas*[1] of Mewat, however, belong to the same ethnic group as the Rajputs, and, in the Persian history- books, wherever the word 'Mewati' occurs, it denotes the very Khanzadas. We, further, learn from Ain-i-Akbari that the Jatau Rajputs came to be known as Mewatis on embracing Islam.

In the annals of Firoz Shahi dynasty, Mewat is mentioned, for the first time, in the memoirs of Shamsuddin Al-timash. The Mewatis had become very troublesome during the early days of the Muslim Kingdom of Delhi. Aided by the long range of thick forests that extended up to Delhi, they used to raid it frequently and had become such a terror that the gates of the capital were shut at sunset. Still, they managed to enter the town in the night in search of plunder, Ghayasuddin Balban, thereupon, despatched a strong military force

---

[1] Denoting the lowest order of Mughal nobility.

against the Mewatis, killing a large number of them. Outposts manned by the Afghan soldiers were set up in Delhi, the surrounding forests were cut down and the land was brought under cultivation, Mewat, thereafter, remained in oblivion for about a hundred years.

After the long lull, the Mewati adventurists, again, became active and started harassing the people of Delhi, which forced the authorities to take punitive action against them from time to time. The names of Bahadur Nahir and his successors are, particularly, mentioned in the chronicles in this connection. They succeeded in establishing the Kingdom of Mewat, which was, later, reduced to a Jagir[1] by the rulers of Delhi.

Another prominent Mewati was Lakhan Pal, who Beginning of the movement of religious reform in Mewat brought the whole of Mewat and its outlying territory under his domination. He embraced Islam during the reign of Firoz Shah.

Moral and religious condition

Owing to the negligence of the Muslim religious teachers, the moral and religious condition of the Mewatis had sunk so low that there was little to distinguish between their beliefs and practices and wholesale apostasy. Even non-Muslim historians have commented at length on their estrangement with Islam, as the following extract from the Alwar Gazetteer of 1878, written by Major Powlett, will show:

> "All the Meos are, now, Muslims, but only in name. Their village, deities are the same as those of the Hindu landlords, and they celebrate several Hindu festivals. Holi is a

[1] Meaning a feudal estate: a fief.

season of special rejoicing among the Mewatis and they observe it like their own festivals, such as, Moharram, 'Id and Shab-i-Barat. The same is the case with Janam Ashtami, Dussehra and Diwali. The Meos engage the services of the Brahmins to fix the dates of marriages. They have Hindu names, with the exception of the word 'Ram', and their last name, often, is 'Singh', though not as frequently as 'Khan'. Like Ahirs and Gujars, the Mewatis, too, observe Amawas as a holiday on which they abstain from work. When they build a well, they begin with the construction of a parapet in the name of Beeriyi or Hanuman, but when it comes to pillage, they do not show much reverence to the Hindu temples and other places of religious significance. If, on such an occasion, their attention is drawn to the sanctity of these establishments, they, unhesitatingly, says, 'You are Does and we are Meos.' Meos are, largely, ignorant of their faith, i.e., Islam. Very few of them know the *Kalima*[1], and fewer still observe Namaz regularly. About the hours and rules of Namaz, their ignorance is complete. This is the state of the Meos of Alwar. In the British territory of Gurgaon, the position is a little better because of the Madrassas. In some parts of Alwar, also, where the mosques have been built, the religious duties are observed to some extent. A few of them know the Kalima and offer up Namaz and an attachment for the Madrassas, also, is found among them. As we have seen earlier, the initial ceremonies of marriage are performed by the Brahmins, but the real ceremony (of Nikah) is performed by the Qazi. Men wear dhoti and loincloth. The pyjamas are not worn at all. Their dress,

---

[1] The Muslim Confessional Formula of *Laa ilaaha illallaah, mohammadur rsoolillah.*

thus, is wholly Hinduised. Even ornaments of gold are worn by men."

At another place, Major Powlett writes

"The meos are half-Hindu by their habits, Mosques are rarely to be seen in their villages. There are only eight mosques in the fifty villages of the Tehsil of *Tijarah*. Leaving aside the temples, the places of worship of the Meos are very much similar to those of their Hindu neighbours. These are known, for instance, as Paanch Peera, Bhaisa and Chahand. Chahand or Khera Deo is consecrated to the service of Maha Devi where animals are offered as a sacrifice. In Shab-i-Barat, the banner of Syed Salar Masud Ghazi is worshipped in all Meo villages."

Similarly, in the Gazetteer of Gurgaon (1910), it is stated that "the Meos, still, are a very loose and careless type of Muslims. They share most of the customs of the neighbouring community, especially those which possess an element of fun and merriment. Their basic rule seems to be to observe the religious celebrations of both communities and disregard the religious duties of either. Lately, some religious teachers have appeared in Mewat, and a few Meos have started to keep the fasts of Ramzan and to build mosques in their villages and observe Namaz. Their women, too, have taken to wearing Pyjamas instead of the Hindu Ghagras[1]. All these are the signs of religious awakening."

The Gazetteer of Bharatpur, again, says:

"The customs of Meos are a mixture of Hindu and Muslim customs. They observe circumcision, perform Nikah, and bury their

---

[1] A garment generally worn by Hindu women, which hangs below the waist and is not parted in the middle.

dead. They make a pilgrimage to the tomb of Syed Salar Masud Ghazi at Bahraich, and attach a great importance to the vow taken under his banner, and consider it a religious duty to fulfil it. They, also, visit the other shrines of India, but do not perform the Haj. Among the Hindu festivals, they celebrate Holi and Diwali. They do not marry in the family or in their own branch or subdivision of the clan, girls do not have a share in ancestral property, and they give mixed Hindu and Muslim names to their children. They are, wholly, illiterate and have a fair number of bards and minstrels among them whom they pay liberally. Many quatrains on he themes of agriculture and rural life are popular which they love to recite. Their speech is rough and coarse, and the manner of addressing both men and women is the same. Intoxicants are widely in use. They are extremely weak of faith and highly superstitious and believe in omens and auguries. Both male and female dresses are Hinduised. In the olden days, infanticide was prevalent, but now it has been given up. Highway robbery and pillage had been their traditional profession, but they have been reformed lately. They, however, are still notorious for cattle-lifting."

Moral virtues

All the same, the Meos are distinguished for some excellent moral qualities and their vices and weaknesses are in the nature of the evil ways and practices that become a part of the moral and social pattern of brave and adventurous races as a result of want of education, isolation from the civilised world and indifference towards religion. These were rampant even among the Arabs during the Age of Ignorance. Natural talents and capabilities had taken a wrong turn owing to the perversity of the environment. Chivalry had degenerated into banditry, manliness had found expression in mutual warfare and bloodshed, sense of pride and self-respect, with no better purpose to serve, had sought fulfilment in the defence of imaginary standards of honour and renown, and high mindedness, for its display had adopted the path of pomp and flourish on petty occasions in the family or clan. In brief, God-given gifts of mind and character were being put to unworthy use, otherwise there was no dearth of virtue and merit among the Meos.

Rugged simplicity, hardihood and firmness of purpose were the chief characteristics of the Mewatis in which they were far superior to the urban Muslim population. It was on account of these qualities that in spite of having drifted so far away from Islam, the floodtide of Apostasy could not submerge the territory of Mewat even in the darkest period of its history.

For centuries the Meos had been living within the shell of their ignorance, keeping by themselves and isolated from the outside world. A parallel can scarcely be found in the Indian history of a community so large and living in such a close proximity to the central seat of power and yet remaining so obscure and isolated. An advantage of it, however, was that the energies of the Mewatis, on the whole, remained conserved, the soil remained virgin while the deplorable habits and customs and superstitious beliefs and practices were, so to speak, like the weeds and scrubs growing on an uncultivated land. The Meos, in the 20th Century, were much like the Arabs in the Age of Perversion.

Beginnings

As we have seen, contact with the Mewatis was established during the lifetime of Maulana Mohammad Ismail. It was not a chance occurrence, but an act of destiny that Maulana Mohammad

Ismail came to live in Basti Nizamuddin which was the gateway of Mewat, and much before the arrival of Maulana Mohammad Ilyas, seeds of loyalty and devotion to his family had been sown on its soil.

When the followers of Maulana Mohammad Ismail and Maulana Mohammad came to know that their true successor, the son of Maulana Mohammad Ismail and the brother of Maulana Mohammad, had come to live at Nizamuddin, they, again, started coming to it and requested Maulana Mohammad Ilyas for a visit so that the old suppliants of his family had an opportunity to renew the ties of fealty and spiritual allegiance.

Real remedy

Maulana Mohammad Ilyas felt that the only way to the religious reform and correction of the Mewatis was the promotion of religious knowledge and familiarisation with the rules and principles of the Shariat.

Maulana Mohammad Ismail, and, after him, Maulana Mohammad had adopted the same method. They used to keep. the Mewati children with them and educate them in their Madrassa, and, then, send them back to Mewat to carry on the work of reform and guidance, and what little religious awareness was found there was owing to the efforts of these pioneers.

Maulana Mohammad Ilyas went a step ahead and decided to establish Maktabs and Madrassas in Mewat itself so that the influence of faith could spread to a wider area and the pace of change was accelerated.

Stipulation

The Maulana knew what was, commonly, meant by inviting a spiritual mentor or his successor to their place by his disciples and admirers, and he was not willing to go to Mewat only to fulfil the formalities of attending the dinner given in his honour, delivering a few sermons and giving good counsel. He wanted to make sure before undertaking the trip, that some real advance would be made, as a result of his visit, towards bringing the Meos closer to Islam and improving their moral condition, and, during those days, the setting up of Maktabs and Madrassas in Mewat appeared to him to be the most effective step in that direction. He had, thus, made it clear that he would accept the invitation only on the condition that they promised to establish Maktabs in their territory.

For the Mewatis, however, no undertaking could be harder to give. They considered the establishment of Maktabs next to impossible for the simple reason that no one would be sending his children. to them, and, thus, depriving himself of their contribution to the family income as daily wage-earners. The enthusiasm of those who came to invite quickly subsided as they heard of the stipulation. In desperation, however, a Mewati, finally, made the promise, leaving the rest to God.

Establishment of Maktabs

Maulana Mohammad Ilyas, accordingly, went to Mewat and demanded the fulfillment of the promise. After great persuasion, the beginning was made and the first Maktabas established.

The Maulana used to tell the Mewatis, "Give me the pupils, I will provide the money." The Meos who were, mainly, farmers, could not easily reconcile themselves to the position that their children applied themselves to reading and writing and stopped working in the fields or looking after the cattle. It took a lot of tact and perseverance to bring them round to it.

Ten Maktabs were opened during that visit. Once the ice was broken, the progress was easy. Sometimes, several Maktabs were opened in a day till, within a few years, hundreds of such schools were functioning in Mewat.

The Maulana had not undertaken the service of faith as a "national cause", the burden of providing the funds for which fell wholly upon the nation or the community, but as a personal affair and felt no hesitation in spending all he had on it. He believed that a person should perform a religious task as his own and expend his time and money freely in its way.

Once, a person presented a purse to him with the request that he use it exclusively for his own needs. The Maulana replied, "If we do not regard Allah's work our own, how can we claim to be His bondmen?" With a sigh, he added, "Alas! We are not just appreciators of the sacred Prophet. We do not know his true worth."

This was the Maulana's rule of life. First of all, he spent from his own pocket on the religious endeavour he had launched in Mewat, and then, alone, would accept help from others.

Chapter IV: Mass effort

With the passage of time, Maulana Mohammad Ilyas became dissatisfied with the progress that was being made, on the individual plane, through the Maktabs. He found that the Maktabs, too, were not free from the effects of the general environment of ignorance and irreligiousness, and the students who passed out of them were incapable of rendering any real service to faith.

There was no genuine attachment to faith, which could induce people to send their children to Maktabs, nor did they know the worth and value of religious knowledge so that recognition could be granted in society to those who acquired it. In such circumstances, the Maktabs could exert little influence on the general pattern of living.

Moreover, all the arrangements were for children who had not yet attained the age of majority, and, thus, were exempted from the application of the commands and injunctions of the Shariat appertaining to religious duties, while there was no provision for the reform and correction of the grown-up people who were incurring the displeasure of the Lord owing to their apathy and ignorance.

Necessary religious instruction could, in any case, not be imparted to the whole of the community in the Maktabs and Madrassas, however large their number. Everyone could not be brought round to attend the Maktabs, nor advised to leave his vocation.

Once, during a tour, a young man was presented before the Maulana with the laudatory remark that he had completed the study of the Quran in such-and-such a Maktab of Mewat. The Maulana was shocked to find that his beard was shaven, and no one could know from his appearance or dress that he was a Muslim. The incident proved too much for his sensitive nature, and he, further, lost his enthusiasm for the Maktabs.

Apart from the setting up of Maktabs, the Maulana, also, tried to settle local disputes and family quarrels, which were very common in Mewat, in the course of his visits. By his tactfulness and high spirituality, he achieved a remarkable success. The Mewatis used to say that "this man is so lean and thin, and yet he finds a solution to whatever problem he takes in hands, and, somehow, even the most strong-headed and obstinate persons submit to his decision without argument."

Some other Ulema, also, took up the task of religious reforms and instruction in Mewat, and, as the Muslim theologians are wont to do in India, they launched a frontal attack on certain widely prevalent un-Islamic practices, Maulana Mohammad Ilyas, However, felt that the condition of faith, at that time, was like that of a flock of sheep: if the herdsman tried to herd the sheep from one side, some of them wandered away from the other side. It would, thus, be futile to attend to the details where the whole life was out of joint. What had departed from the hearts was the awareness of faith itself.

Repeated experience had convinced him that the real remedy, of the malaise did not lie in individual correction or in confining the approach to the upper classes of the society. As a simple Mewati had, once, said, "Nothing can be done until Faith is taken to the Masses."

Second Haj and new direction of Movement

Maulana Mohammad Ilyas left for the second Haj in April 1925, in the company of Maulana Khalil Ahmad Saharanpuri. When the period of stay in Madina drew to a close and the companions of Maulana Mohammad Ilyas got ready to leave, they noticed a peculiar restlessness in him. He did not want to depart. After a few days, the companions reported it to Maulana Khalil Ahmad who advised them not to insist upon the Maulana to leave, but to wait till he himself decided to return with them. Or else, they could depart and let the Maulana remain behind as long as he wanted. The companions decided to stay.

Maulana Mohammad Ilyas used to say that "during the stay at Madina I was commanded to this work and it was said to me that 'I shall take the work from you.' For a few days, I was very worried. I did not know what a weak and helpless man like me could do. I, then, related it to a pious and sagacious person who remarked that there was no need to be anxious. What I had been told was not to carry out the task but that the task would be taken from me. He who was to take the service would do it in whatever way he pleased."

The Maulana felt very much relieved at the reply and left Madina for home. In all, he stayed for about five months in the holy cities of Mecca and Madina and returned to Kandhla in September 1925.

Tabligh tours

On coming back from the Haj, Maulana Mohammad Ilyas began the *Tabligh*[1] tours and called upon others, also, to come

[1] Meaning preaching and propagation of Islam.

forward and propagate the fundamental tenets of Islam, like Kalima and Namaz, directly among the masses. People, on the whole, were unfamiliar with such a thing. They had never heard of it before and were reluctant to respond to the call. With great difficulty, a few persons were persuaded to join the Movement. At a public meeting in Nooh, the Maulana explained his call and urged upon the people to organise themselves in *Jama'ats*[1] and go out countryside to spread the teachings of Islam. They asked for a month's time, after which a *Jama'at* was formed, and the villages they were to visit during the first eight days were decided upon and it was agreed that they would offer the next Friday prayers at Sohna'in the Gurgaon district where the programme for the next week would be chalked out.

The party, hence, offered the congregational prayers on the first Friday at Sohna. The Maulana, also, came and the programme for the next week was settled. The *Jama'at*, again, set out on the tour and the next Friday service was celebrated at Tauroo and the third at Nagina in the tehsil of Ferozepur. The Maulana joined the party at each place and the plan for the next week was drawn in consultation with him.

For several years the *Tabligh* work was done, along those lines, in Mewat and appeals were made to the men of theological institutions, at public meeting organised by the *Tabligh* parties, to extend their active co-operation.

Third Haj

The Maulana performed the third Hajj in 1932. The Ramzan moon having been sighted at Nizamuddin, the *Taraweeh* prayers

[1] Meaning a party or group.

were offered at the Delhi Railway Station, after which the party boarded the train for Karachi. Writing from Mecca, Maulana Ihtishamul Hasan, who had accompanied the Maulana on the Pilgrimage, said in a letter to Sheikhul Hadees Maulana Mohammad Zakaria that "most of Maulana's time is spent in Harem[1], *Tabligh* meetings and discussions are frequently held, and the Maulana makes it a point to say something about his endeavour everywhere."

The Maulana returned to India with renewed enthusiasm and a greater faith in his mission. He accelerated the pace of the work and undertook two tours of Mewat with a large body of companions. At least a hundred persons remained with him throughout the tours, and, at some places, the crowd was much larger. The first tour lasted for a month while the other, a few days less. During the tours, *Jama'ats* were formed, and villages were allotted to them for doing the rounds and preaching the Word of God.

Towards religious centres

Maulana Mohammad Ilyas had realised that it was very difficult for the poor Mewati peasants to spare time for religious education, nor could one expect their lives to be transformed in the little time they could devote. It was, also, unreasonable to hope that all of them would join the Maktabs and Madrassas. Yet they had to be brought out of the life of Ignorance and made safe for Islam. The only way to it, in Maulana's view, was to persuade them to go, in *Jama'ats*, to the religious centres and spend some time there preaching the Kalima and Namaz to the common people, and, thus, perfecting the knowledge they had acquired of faith, and sitting in

---

[1] The sacred enclosure at Mecca in which the House of K'aba is situated.

the company of the theologians and spiritual mentors of the place, listening to their conversation and observing their deportment and behaviour, and, in that manner, learning about Islam by the direct method and in the natural way. Besides, in those days than which they could, apparently, not hope to have a more undisturbed time, they were to concentrate on reading the Quran, learning the commands of the Shariat and listening to the life-accounts of the holy Companions so that they returned home from the Madrassa in a much-improved state.

But it was a most difficult and delicate task. No religious leader or spiritual guide had, perhaps, made such a demand from his followers. To make people leave their homes and give up their vocations, even temporarily, was not easy, particularly when they had only recently acquired the awareness of Faith.

Another difficulty was that one could not be sure how would the peasant-preachers be received at those places. Would their ignorance, simplicity and coarseness of language and manners be treated with indulgence or scorn?

The Maulana considered the Western part of the United Provinces (now Uttar Pradesh)- comprising of the districts of Muzaffarnagar and Saharanpur, which he, sometimes, described as Doaba, and, sometimes, straightaway as U.P. the well-spring of Faith and the seat of godly men. No other place could, in his opinion, be more suitable for seeking the company of the virtuous and venerable servants of the Lord and acquiring the knowledge of faith directly through the eyes and the ears.

He was convinced that ignorance, listlessness and emotional instability lay at the root of the trouble and the safest and most practical method to counteract them was that the Mewatis went to the religious centres of Western U.P., for instruction and inspiration.

In a letter to a friend, the Maulana wrote: "Ignorance and listlessness in the sphere of religious endeavour is the source of all mischief, and God knows how many evils you will see taking their rise from people remaining at that deplorable moral and religious level and will not be able to do anything about it. For overcoming the evils that are already there and barring the door for those which may threaten to arise in future, you have no other option but to prevail upon the people to go to the United Provinces and act according to the plan that has been set into operation in your region."

The Maulana, also, hoped that his movement would, thus, come under the benign shadow of the Ulema and godly men of those areas. They would get an opportunity to obtain a firsthand knowledge of the pathetic state of the poor and isolated Muslims of Mewat and it might strike a sympathetic chord in their hearts and make them favourably inclined towards them. The patronage of the pious souls was essential, according to the Maulana. Without it, the *Tabligh* endeavour would not bear fruit.

Kandhla - the first choice

The Maulana's choice for the first place to be visited fell upon Kandhla. It was his hometown, and the people with whom the *Tabligh* men would come into contact were his kinsmen. Moreover, it was a well-known religious and educational centre of the Muslims.

In the month of Ramzan, the Maulana told his colleagues to prepare men for going to Kandhla. It seemed unbelievable for the rustics of Mewat to go for *Tabligh* to a place like Kandhla which, above all, was the home of Maulana Mohammad Ilyas's own preceptor. The response, therefore, was very discouraging, and even a sincere adherent like Haji Abdur Rahman expressed his inability to make the trip as it was the village of his teacher, Maulana Mohammad.

But it was not the Maulana's habit to say a thing without giving serious consideration to it. He put the whole force of his personality behind the problem at hand, and his friends and associates could not easily decline to do what he wanted.

A party of ten Mewatis, at last, left Delhi for Kandhla, after the 'Id service, under the leadership of Hafiz Maqbool Hasan.

Within a few days of it, the Maulana decided to take another party to Raipur, which, too, was a safe place and a religious and spiritual centre: Because of his close association with Maulana Abdul Qadir, the successor of Shah Abdur Rahim Raipuri, it was like a second home to him.

An incident worth recalling here is that the child of Qari Dawood, who was to be one of the members of the *jama'at*, died on the day of departure. Qari Saheb buried the child and started on the tour directly from the graveyard, without caring to go home and console his family.

Organised tours of Mewat

Maulana Mohammad Ilyas had maps prepared of all the Tehsils of Mewat and the district of Gurgaon. He chalked out the routes for the *Tabligh* parties and instructed them to maintain a daily record of their activities. The community-wise population of every village visited and the distance between one village and another were to be noted down as well as the names of the bigger villages of the neighbourhood and their Numberdars.

At a meeting at Chitaura, in the district of Ferozepur, 16 parties were organised, each with an Amir[1] and an Amirul Umara[2], who was to be in charge of 4 Amirs. These parties were to undertake the tour of the entire territory of Mewat with the arrangement that four of them were to tour the hilly areas, four of the villages situated between the main roads and the hills, four of the villages between the road leading from Howdal and Alwar to Delhi, and four of the villages lying between the Jamuna River and the road leading from Delhi to Howdal. At each halting place, someone came from Nizamuddin to collect the news and address the meeting. All the sixteen *Tabligh* parties collected at Faridabad where the Maulana, also, came and a meeting was held. At Faridabad, the sixteen parties were merged into four, which came to Ja'ma Masjid, Delhi by different routes, and, after a public meeting there, proceeded to Panipat, Sonipat etc., etc.,

Meanwhile, efforts at persuading the people to set out of their homes for learning the faith continued in Mewat. It had now become the passion of Maulana's life. Numerous tours of Mewat were made and public meetings were organised. Everywhere, he put forward the same idea in different ways and with different inducements and urged upon the people to dedicate their lives to the *Tabligh* endeavour for it, alone, held the key to their religious and worldly advancement till the Herculian task began to look less frightening.

---

[1] Meaning leader.

[2] The leader of leaders.

More and more *Jama'ats* were formed for *Tabligh* tours within and outside Mewat and stress was laid on making the *Tabligh* movement as popular as any other movement in the country. Rallies and meetings were organised at suitable places, and on all such occasions, a few new *Jama'ats* were formed which set out for various destinations. People began to donate time for *Tabligh*. Donations of money were common in the world, but a new trend was set in Mewat-that of donating time-weeks and months for the cause of faith.

The Maulana aimed at the generation of the spirit of dedication and sacrifice for the sake of Islam. He wanted the *Tabligh* workers to attain the stage where they could suffer the loss in trade or agriculture willingly. It was after much hard work that the beginning was made in Mewat towards habitually subordinating the material interests to the higher aims and ideals of the religious endeavour.

Popular upsurge

The tremendous change that came over Mewat as a result of the untiring efforts of *Tabligh* workers who moved from village to village, carrying their luggage on their backs, is, perhaps, without a parallel in recent times. Within a few years, the whole region emerged from darkness into light. Had a government, with all its resources in men and material, tried to bring the people nearer to Faith, it would not have achieved so much in such a short time.

The ideal method of the preaching and propagation of faith, indeed, was what was witnessed during the earliest phase of Islam when Muslim crusaders brought their own arms and other provisions and fought solely out of love for martyrdom and eagerness to earn the countenance of the Lord. The preachers and other functionaries of the State, too, discharged their duties not for remuneration's sake, but as the servants of God. In the *Tabligh* endeavour of Mewat, one could see a glimpse of those marvellous times. Anyone who saw the *Tabligh* parties of Mewat, travelling on foot, with blankets thrown on their shoulders, the *siparas* tucked under the arms and parched grain or bread tied in a corner of the mantle, their tongues engaged in Zikr, eyes showing the signs of nightly vigil and the mark of Sajda on the foreheads would have been reminded of the martyred Companions of the Bir Ma'ona[1] who were killed while going on the mission of teaching the Quran and imparting the knowledge of the commandments of the Shariat on the orders of the holy Prophet.

Resistance to change gave place to readiness to responds to the call of faith, and it was, no longer, necessary for *Tabligh* workers to strive and struggle at each step. Though there was still much to be done (and some undesirable practices are prevalent even today), what was needed now in the areas in which the spade-work had been done was only to tell the people that such was the command of God and the Prophet and the requirement of Islam and they would fall in line with it.

According to the Maulana, the correct approach was to enkindle the spark of faith in the hearts and engender a genuine urge for Islam and a living awareness of its worth which could persuade the people to incur the loss of life and property in this world for the sake of the reward of the Hereafter. The inclination

---

[1] The holy Prophet had sent 70 Muslims on a religious mission, but when they reached the place called Bir Ma'ona, the tribesmen ambushed the party, killing all its members save K'ab bin Zayd.

and ability to follow the Islamic way of life and abide by the rules of the Shariat would, then, be produced automatically.

The gains of religiousness began to appear in Mewat which would not have, otherwise, been possible even after long years of struggle. Thousands of mosques were built where not one was to be seen for miles, and innumerable Maktabs and Arabic Madrassas were established. The number of *Huffaz*[1] increased to over a hundred and so did that of qualified *Alim*[2]. A dislike for Hinduised garments was created and people began to dress themselves according to the specification of the Shariat. Bracelets got removed from the arms and rings from the ears of men. Beards were grown freely and without compulsion. Polytheistic ceremonies that had become a part of marriage began to discard. Usury lost its hold, drinking almost came to an end and crimes became less frequent. Religious indifference and innovations and lewd and profane habits and customs started to wither away in the new climate of faith and piety.

When an elderly Mewati known by the name of Qari Dawood was asked what was happening in his land, he replied: "All that I know is that things for which great efforts were made in the past, but there was nothing to show are now taking place automatically and things to stop which great efforts were made and even battles were fought in the past, but not one of them could be eradicated are now disappearing by themselves."

All this, in Maulana's view, was the direct outcome of setting out in the path of faith, and, particularly, of making regular visits to the religious centres of Western U.P., In a letter to a Mewati, he wrote: "Such are the effects of the visits by the *Jama'ats* to U.P.,

---

[1] Plural of Hafiz, meaning one who has the whole of the Quran by heart.

[2] Meaning theological scholars.

though only a small number of men make them, and the figure had not yet reached the mark of two hundred, and the time spent there is very little as compared to what is spent at home. People have begun to talk of the Great Revolution in this brief period and the unholy sentiments of the people of your region who were steeped in ignorance have begun to change into the noble sentiments of spreading the faith."

Nevertheless, he felt sure that if the Mewatis did not make the *Tabligh* tours a way of life and ceased to make an earnest endeavour for faith, they would slip back not only into the former condition, but even worse. Owing to the religious awakening, the eyes of the world were turned towards Mewat, but there were as many mischiefs as the eyes. The need for vigilance was greater now that the barrier of isolation had been broken. In a letter, he said: "Unless you devote yourself whole-heartedly to persuading your people to travel from one place to another continuously for as many as four months for the sake of *Tabligh*, the community will not have a real taste of Faith and religiousness. What has been achieved so far is purely transitory and if you give up the endeavour, the condition of the community will become even worse than what it was. The isolation, so far, was acting as a bullwork, on account of which the other communities did not take notice of the Mewatis. But now if the community does not protect itself, it will fall a prey to their wicked intentions."

Traditional preachers

Maulana Mohammad Ilyas had engaged some paid preachers at Delhi and a few other places who carried on for about two and a half years, but the Maulana was dissatisfied with the progress they were making. He felt that the goal he had set before himself could not be attained like that. The sense of movement generated through the efforts of the selfless workers of Mewat and the results their revolutionary approach was producing were not possible by the slow and lifeless mode of functioning of the traditional preachers. The Maulana, therefore, decided to do away with paid workers.

Last Hajj

It was an ardent desire of the Maulana to go with some of his close associates to the citadel of Islam, i.e., Arabia, after the Movement had acquired solidity in India, and give the Call of *Tabligh* in the land from where Islam had sprung up and sent forth its blossoms all over the world. "Didn't the people of Arabia deserve more than anyone else that the priceless gifts was taken back to them?" he asked. The desire grew with the passage of time and became irresistible till, in 1938, he, again, left for the Haj with a large party of trusted colleagues including Maulana Ihtishmul Hasan, Molvi Mohammad Yusuf, Molvi Inamul Hasan and Haji Abdur Rahman. On the ship, the Maulana devoted himself to *Tabligh* and to the teaching of the rites and ceremonies of the Haj, and during the journey from Jedda to Mecca, addressed a gathering of the noblemen of Bahra. As the days of the Haj were near and boarding and lodging arrangements, also, had to be made, the Maulana could not pay much attention to *Tabligh* in Mecca, but at Mina he, frequently, met the pilgrims coming from different countries and had prolonged discussions with them, and, also, addressed a public meeting.

On the completion of the Haj, the Maulana consulted some leading Indian pilgrims about extending the *Tabligh* movement to

Arabia, but they stoutly opposed it on the ground that the conditions obtaining in Arabia, at that time, did not warrant it. He, then, sought the advice of Maulana Shafiuddin who enthusiastically supported the idea and said that he felt sure help would come from the Lord.

The Maulana held lengthy discussions with a party of pilgrims from Bahrain who promised to take up the *Tabligh* work on their return. He, also, had long talks with some prominent Muslim merchants who had settled in Arabia. At first, they took an alarming view of the proposal, but after a few meetings, their attitude softened, and they agreed to co- operate. They, however, suggested that the permission of King Ibn-i-Saud should, first, be obtained and it was decided that the aims and objects were to be written in Arabic and presented to the King.

After about two weeks, on March 14, 1938, the Maulana called upon Sultan Ibn-i-Saud along with Haji Abdullah Dehlavi, Abdur Rahman Mazhar and Molvi Ihtishamul Hasan. The Sultan stepped down from his *masnad*[1] to receive them and, for forty minutes, gave learned discourse on Divine Unity, the Quran and the Sunnah, and on the need to follow the Shariat, and when they were ready to leave, he, again, came down from the *masnad* to bid them farewell. On the next day, the Sultan left for Riad.

A memorandum prepared by Maulana Ihtishamul Hasan in Arabic was sent to *Raisul-Quzzat* (Chief Justice) Abdullah bin Hasan, and then, the Maulana saw him personally. The Raisul-Quzzat, too, received him with great honour and expressed agreement with his

---

[1] Meaning a throne, a large cushion or couch.

proposal, but said that the permission could be given only by Amir Feisal.[1]

Throughout the stay in Mecca, A *Jama't* went out Daily, both in the morning and the evening, on *Tabligh* mission and made direct, personal contacts with the people. A few meetings, also, were held at which Molvi Mohammad Idris and Molvi Nur Mohammad spoke in Urdu, and, the ground was, thus, prepared for going forward with the task.

The Maulana had impressed upon his companions in the Haj that at that time and at that place, *Tabligh* was more important the Umra[2] or any other act of worship.

It is related by the Maulana's son, Maulana Mohammad Yusuf, that "once we were sitting in our apartment near Babul Umra and the Maulana was saying something and we were listening that a stranger came and stood in front of the door and said, 'Go on with the work you are doing. The reward on it is so great that if was revealed to you, you would die of joy.' He then, went away and we could not know who he was. The Maulana kept on talking and took no notice of the incident."

On arriving at Medina from Mecca, the Maulana learnt that the Governor of Medina was not empowered to grant the permission for the *Tabligh* movement. He would forward the papers to Mecca and await the instructions.

Discussions continued with different people and the Maulana twice visited Qubba where he, also, addressed a public meeting and a few persons offered their services. He went twice to

---

[1] The Viceroy of the king Hejaz.

[2] The Pilgrimage to Mecca at any time of the year other than that of the Haj.

Ohad[1] where Molvi Nur Mohammad and Molvi Mohammad Yusuf spoke at a meeting in Arabic and were heard with interest. Bedouins, too, were contacted, children were asked to pronounce the Kalima, and frequent visits were paid to Ribat[2]. As for the main objective of *Tabligh*, the prospects, sometimes, appeared bright, and, sometimes, gloomy, but one thing was certain: there was a greater need of *Tabligh* in Arabia than in India.

Return

The Maulana remained constantly in touch with the progress of the Movement in Mewat and Delhi. Letters giving details of the work were regularly received from India, and he sent back the necessary instructions.

On the advice of friends, the Maulana decided to return to India after a fortnight's stay in Medina. Shedding light on the decision, he wrote to a well-wishes in Mecca that "the reason for coming back (to India) was that as after a fortnight's stay in Medina, I drew attention, one morning, at tea to the ways of launching the Movement with full force and on firm foundations, all the friends who were known for soundness of judgement, positively, told me that, for it, at least two years' stay was needed. I agreed with them, but it was, also, clear that if I remained away from India for such a long time, what had been achieved there would be lost. The aim, therefore, is to put the *Tabligh* work in India on such lines that I can devote myself single-mindedly to the task in Arabia. I have come

---

[1] Situated at about three kilometres to the north of Medina. It was here that the second battle was fought against the Pagans of Mecca in the third year of Hijrah.

[2] Literally, an hotel, an inn, a caravanserai Here it denotes a place where the Haj pilgrims are lodged.

back with the intention of a temporary stay. If you are really interested in the preservation of Islam, and the faith of Mohammad is more valuable to you than the other engagements, and my approach, also, is correct in your sight, then strengthen your faith through an earnest and wholehearted dedication to the *Tabligh* endeavour."

Chapter V:
Stabilisation of the movement in Mewat - and its Expansion

On returning to India, Maulana Mohammad Ilyas intensified *Tabligh* activities in Mewat. A large number of tours were carried out, door-to-door campaigns were launched, and public meetings were organised. Once again, *Tabligh* parties began to arrive at Basti Nizamuddin and groups of Mewatis started visiting the districts of Western U.P., Approach was made to the urban classes of Muslims, and the Movement was extended to Delhi as well on the same lines as in Mewat. *Tabligh Jama'ats* were formed in Mohallas and the weekly rounds were commenced.

Impulsion's

The Maulana had drawn the following conclusions from what he had seen and experienced in the urban areas:

1) There did exist religiousness in the towns, but its frontiers were shrinking. It had disappeared from among the masses, at first, and then, Stabilization of the Movement in Mewat and Its expansion receded further till only a few persons remained who acted upon the tenets of faith and observed piety as a duty. Now, religiousness had ceased to be a social force and was found only on the individual level and the number of such individuals. Too, was dwindling day by day. In some cases, of course, it was present in a high degree, which was very pleasing, and one felt grateful that even in these times such wonderful specimens of

righteousness and good doing were to be seen, but they were becoming scarce and it was feared that with the passing away of these warmly devoted servants of the Lord, religiousness would disappear from the world altogether.

The Maulana had witnessed a pitiable decline in his own lifetime. Families and towns which were the cradles of guidance and where the lamps of learning and instruction had been burning for centuries were presenting a spectacle of degeneration. There was no one to take the place of the man of God who died. The Maulana was, personally, aware of the moral and spiritual decay that had set in and around Muzaffarnagar, Saharanpur and Delhi, and it made him sad. In a letter of Condolence, he wrote: "Alas! Those who take delight in the Name of God are no longer born, and those who have attained some heights in the blessed company of devout are departing from the world without leaving anyone to take their place."

The Maulana had only one remedy to offer: the taking of the faith to the masses. Then, alone, could the environment be generated that gave rise to men of exceptional virtue and spirituality. So had it been in the past, and in the present times, as well, no progress could be made without it.

2) Muslims who lived in the cities and led a busy life had presumed that there was a great deal of hardship in religion. They believed that Faith meant withdrawal from the world, which was not practicable. Having, thus, despaired of religion, they had plunged headlong into worldly affairs and interests,

and resigned themselves to a wholly materialistic and un-Islamic way of life.

Things, indeed, had gone so far that when the attention of the Muslims was drawn to their religious responsibilities, they, unashamedly, said, "We are worldly people. We are the slaves of the stomach and the dogs of the world."

Clearly, it was a woeful misconception. Faith meant nothing but to lead one's life and pursue one's worldly activities in accordance with the Shariat, which any Muslims could do in the midst of his mundane occupations. What was needed was only a little heedfulness and some religious knowledge. The misunderstanding must be removed if the mournful march of Muslims towards irreligiousness was to be arrested.

In a letter, the Maulana wrote: "The general concept of the world is highly erroneous. Worldliness does not denote pursuit of the means of livelihood. There is the curse of God. on the world, and God does not enjoin or give the command of a thing upon which is His curse. Thus, to engage in a thing for which the command has been given, realising that it was the command of God, and paying due heed to what is allowed and what is forbidden is in respect of it, is faith, while to ignore the command and determine one's needs on one's own or regard them as essential on any other ground, aside of the command, is worldliness."

The Maulana, sometimes, likened faith to the Saliva without which no food could be digested nor its taste perceived. Everyone possessed a sufficient quantity of it. In the same way, every Muslim possessed a sufficient quantity of faith. He had, simply, to mix it with his worldly aims and interests, and then, the world, too, for him, would become Faith.

3) It had come to be believed about religious education that it could be acquired only through books and in the Arabic Madrassas and as everyone could not study in a Madrassa for 8 or 10 years, the common Muslims had concluded that they were not fated to acquire religious knowledge and resigned themselves to spending their lives in ignorance.

True as it was that religious knowledge was acquired in Arabic Madrassas, it implied the advanced grade of it, which was neither necessary nor possible for all Muslims. Every Muslim, however, could obtain the requisite knowledge amidst his worldly pre-occupations. The holy Companions, with the exception of a small group of Ahl-i- Suffa, had their families and vocations to look after. They were traders, peasants and artisans, and had their own worries and problems. There was no Arabic theological Madrassa, in the modern sense, in Medina, and even if there was one, they could not spend 8 or 10 years in it. Yet, as everyone knew, they possessed the necessary knowledge of faith and were not unaware of its essential teachings. How, then, had they learnt it all? By keeping the company of the Prophet, and sitting with those who knew, and associating freely with men of Faith and observing their actions, and, by going along with them in journeys and on Jehad and inquiring from them about the correct religious position when a need arose. An opportunity of that class or standard was not available now, but something comparable to it, in some degree, could, certainly, be done which was that the Muslims who led a busy life and were engrossed in their trades or professions, and the city-dwellers, on the whole, were persuaded to set aside some of their time for gaining the knowledge of faith, and, thus, pay Zakat, for the sake of God, on their hours, days and years, as they did on their wealth. They should be urged upon to come out of the environment in which, as experience had shown, no perceptible change could be brought about in their lives, nor even a rudimentary knowledge of faith obtained in spite of the desire. One still was at the same level of ignorance at which one was twenty or twenty-five years ago, and if the Namaz of a person was defective, it had remained like that for years, and whoever did not know the *Qunoot*[1] or the prayer of the funeral service was even now ignorant of it, though they had listened to hundreds of sermons, and lived, for a long time, in the neighbourhood of theologists and thousands of religious books had been written and sold in the market. If all went to show that though it might be logically feasible for a man to reform himself in those surroundings, in the world of reality it did not happen.

It was, therefore, essential that, for a time, people were brought out of the static and irreligious environment and enabled to dwell in an entirely different climate, away from the affairs and interests of everyday life.

4) The true design and structure of a Muslim's life demanded of him to take an active part in the service of faith or that he aided those who were engaged in it, and, at the same time, aspired to participate directly in such activities though, for the time being, he was unable to do so for one reason or the other. The city-life, which the Maulana described as a life of ease as compared to that of struggle and exertion in the path of God, was aimless and unrelated to the ideals of Islam. It was a soulless, work-a-day existence which was confined to earning and spending. The Maulana wanted the city-dwellers to adopt a life of "assistance and migration", i.e., of toil and sacrifice

---

[1] A special prayer of repentance and obeisance recited in the Namaz of Witr.

for the sake of faith. He did not believe in the division of labour with some people serving the cause of God and other looking after their own worldly affairs. It was altogether wrong and foolish to rest content with giving financial help to those who strove in the path of Faith and imagine that the propagation and preservation of Islam was the duty of the Ulema alone.

The Maulana used to say that just as the division of the functions of life was not possible-it could not be that while one person ate, the other drank and the third clothed himself, in the same way, it was essential for everyone to observe the duties of faith, gain a requisite knowledge of its rules and doctrines, and make some effort for the supremacy of the Word of God along with looking after his economic and other worldly interests.

Stay of Mewatis in Delhi

Maulana Mohammad Ilyas, thus, regarded the *Tabligh* movement highly important for the city-dwelling Muslims and wanted to give the call to them with all the strength at his command. According to him, to deliver a sermon or to write a book was not only not enough, but could, also, be harmful without solid work and a reliable life-example. In a letter he wrote: "Unless there is a practical example before the people, speeches from the pulpit cannot arouse them to action. If a plan of work did not follow the speeches, the people will not take the speeches seriously."

The Maulana began to send parties of Mewatis to Delhi and other important centres where they stayed for a long time. At first, they had to face enormous difficulties. They were not allowed to spend the nights in the mosques, and if they, somehow, managed to stay in a mosque, various impediments were placed in their way.

They could not, for instance, use the lavatory. Threats were hurled at them, and they were abused. But gradually, the things changed and as people were convinced of the sincerity and selflessness of the Mewatis, they began to treat them with kindness.

Educated Classes

The Maulana felt that the active co-operation of the religious and educated classes was essential to the success of the Movement. He did not want only their vocal support, through sermons and speeches, but that the Ulema, actually, combined in the effort and went from door to door in the manner of the pious precursors. In a letter to Sheikhul Hadees Maulana Mohammad Zakaria, he remarked:

> "I have long been of the view that unless educated persons called at the door of the common people and went from town to town and village to village like ordinary men, the Movement would not be successful because learned and forceful discourses of the Ulema could not have the same effect on the masses as their physical participation. This, as you will be aware, is evident, also, from the lives of our precursors."

Often it was said that if the teachers and the students of the Madrassas associated themselves actively with the *Tabligh* movement their work would suffer, but the arrangement the Maulana had in mind was such that it assured their mental and educational advancement. As he, once, wrote:

> "Faith can progress only in proportion to and under the shadow of educational advancement. It will be a great loss

to me if education suffered in the least owing to the *Tabligh* movement. I do not, at all, want to discourage do harm to those who are gaining knowledge by study. They must, on the other hand, make much greater progress for the extent to which they are making the progress now 1S most unsatisfactory."

What he desired was that, in the *Tabligh* movement, the students learnt, under the supervision of their own teachers, to do justice to their education and serve the mankind through it so that their education was beneficial to others as well. He observed, "May it be so that the students received training in the sanctioning of what was right and forbidding of what was wrong under the guidance of their teachers during the schooldays. Only then can education be useful. As the case is, at present, it is being wasted and helping the forces of Ignorance and Perversion."

Guidelines

The Maulana sent parties of Mewatis to Deoband, Saharanpur, Raipur and Thana Bhawan with the definite instructions to abstain from talking about *Tabligh* in the assemblies of religious and spiritual mentors. They were to make a tour of the adjoining villages in groups of 50 or 60, and return to the town on the 8th day, and then, again, fan out into the villages. If the religious leaders enquired from them about their activities, they were to tell them, otherwise not. In a letter to Maulana Mohammad Zakaria, he wrote:

"For a long time, I have been wanting that the *Jama'ats* went to the spiritual mentors, and, observing the proprieties of the Sufi-lodges, availed themselves of the advantages of staying there, and, also, undertook the *Tabligh* tours of the adjoining villages, according to a fixed programme. Please chalk out the plan for it in consultation with the men who are coming. Most probably, 1, too, will come, with some colleagues, during the week. I intend to go to Deoband and Thana Bhawan also."

Dispelling of fears and misgivings

Fears and misgivings of a number of Ulema and spiritual leaders as regards the *Tabligh* Movement were dispelled owing to strict compliance with these principles.

Take, for instance, the case of Thana Bhawan. The *Tabligh Jama'ats* toured its neighbouring areas and made a direct contact with the common people, and as visitors from those places came to Maulana Ashraf Ali Thanwi, They told him about the good work the *Tabligh* workers were doing. In the beginning, the Maulana was skeptical. What illiterate Mewatis could do when the Ulema who had studied in the Arabic Madrassàs for 8 or 10 years had failed to make a headway and ended up only in giving rise to multitudinous evils, he thought. He was afraid that Maulana Mohammad Ilyas's style of *Tabligh* would lead to disaster. But his fears were removed as the reports of the progress the Mewatis were making poured in and he, also, personally, felt the. favourable effects of their endeavours. Thus, once when Maulana Mohammad Ilyas wanted to discuss his plan of work with him, he observed, "It is needless to argue. Reasons can be given for or against anything. I have been convinced by the actual work that is being done. No further proof or discussion is needed. You have turned despair into hope."

Indifference of the educated classes

Maulana Mohammad Ilyas's faith in his mission was boundless. It made him sad that the educated classes did not take a genuine interest in it. Day by day, the conviction had grown in him that the religious endeavour he had begun.

held the real answer to the ills and evils that were plaguing the Muslim Millet. Whenever a new mischief cropped up, his ardour and enthusiasm reasserted itself with a greater force. At a moment like it, he wrote to the head of a premier theological institution:

> "I do not know. with what intensity to explain and with what tongue to speak, and, above all, with what force to fix it in my mind and how to make a known thing unknown, and an unknown thing known. I am positive that there is no other way to build the wall of Alexander against the high tide of these vices and mischiefs than to associate energetically and whole-heartedly with the Movement I have started. The emergence of the Movement from nowhere shows that it is the remedy, for is it not the practice of the Lord that He produces the cure when an epidemic has broken out? It never does good to disregard a boon or remedy sent by God." In the same way, in another letter, he said:

> "I do not know how to express the agony with which I am writing this letter. My friend, clearly and intensely as I see the propinquity, good pleasure and help of the Lord as a result of joining this Movement, so, also, do I fear that the failure to show proper warmth and respect. to such a distinguished guest from Above might lead to infliction and misfortune."

The Maulana suffered in silence, and, as far as possible, did not reveal his feelings to anyone. It was not his habit to find fault with others. When anyone complained to him about the apathy and indifference of the Ulema, he would, simply, say, "When you cannot leave your interests and activities about which you know that these are worldly, how can these gentlemen leave their interests and activities about which they believe that these are religious? When you cannot leave the shop, how can you expect them to leave the masnad? Why should you, then, have a grudge against them?"

Causes

Some of the causes of the indifference and inattention were:

i) Those were the days of agitation's and upheavals, and people were mostly interested in them. In such conditions, it was difficult for the quiet and constructive endeavour of the Maulana to evoke an enthusiastic response. Moreover, the past experience of *Tabligh* movement had not been very encouraging.

ii) Very little was known about the nature of the Maulana's work, and apart from those who were closely associated with it, few people among the educated classes-specially the distantly places ones had an idea of it. The Maulana avoided publicity.

iii) The term *'Tabligh'* by which the Movement was popularly known, also, proved a handicap. People were inclined to dismiss it as superficial and fanciful.

iv) The Maulana himself was its sole advocate before the Ulema and the difficulty with him was that, often, his speech became confused owing to the originality of ideas and the intensity of feeling, and, also, because of his habit of stuttering.

Further, the ideas, at times, were so sublime that they were not to be found in the standard books, and were, also, expressed in a non-technical language due to which the Ulema, generally, did not feel drawn towards the Movement.

v) The Ulema were not expected to form a very high opinion of the Maulana from the rustic Mewatis whose religious leader he was commonly supposed to be.

Inner burning

Nevertheless, the inner burning of the Maulana was, no, eager to spread out and the time had come for the Movement to forge ahead. The pre-occupation of Maulana. Mohammad Ilyas with the *Tabligh* call had been growing steadily: newer aspects of it were being revealed to him and their sources discovered in the Quran and Sunnah and in the life-accounts of the holy Prophet and the Companions. On the other hand, to listen to those profound truths were, mostly, the simple-minded Mewatis who were not even conversant with the literary language of the Maulana or the technical terms of the Shariat and Tasawwuf.

Spiritually, however, the Mewatis were very much suited to the task. They were far more virile and energetic than the Ulema and the city-dwellers and were the products of 20 years of unceasing struggle. They formed the backbone of the Movement. The Maulana acknowledged it freely, as the following extract from a letter to Mewati friends would show: "I have spent my energy on you and I can do nothing but to sacrifice you even further. Join hands with me."

Similarly, on another occasion, he said:

"There are many to devote themselves to worldly pursuits, but at present, God has decreed it only for the Mewatis to set out of their homes for the sake of faith."

In and around Saharanpur

The teachers of the Madrassa of Mazaahirul Uloom of Saharanpur were closest to the Maulana. Maulana Mohammad Zakaria, and the secretary of its managing Committee, Maulana Hafiz Abdul Latif, and other members of its staff frequently attended the Tabligh meetings in Mewat and would come to Nizamuddin whenever the Ma wanted. But the Maulana was not satisfied with it. He desired much greater involvement and with that end in view, turned the attention of *Tabligh* parties, particularly, towards Saharanpur, and, personally, undertook the tours of the adjoining villages, such as, Behat, Mirzapur and Salempur with the teachers of Mazaahirul Uloom.

In 1940, it was decided that the chain of *Tabligh* parties to Saharanpur should not be broken, when one *Jama'at* was to return, another should go there to take its place. For a year, they used to stay in the building of the Madrassa, and then, a house was taken on rent, but it had to be vacated after a few months. It went on like that for 4 years. The illiterate Mewatis were, sometimes, treated with scant respect and it was asked how they could discharge the duty of religious instruction and reform when they stood in need of it themselves. The Maulana warned against the misconception. He said, "Do not regard these people (the Mewatis) the reformers. Learn only this thing from them: the leaving of one's home for the advancement of faith; and, in all other matters, consider them to be dependent on you. You criticise them because of the presumption that they are the reformers."

Beyond Delhi and Mewat

Gradually, the *Tabligh* movement began to be talked about outside Mewat and Delhi, and a few articles on it, also, appeared in reputed journals. People who cherished a vague desire to serve in the faith were encouraged by the reports and they met Maulana Mohammad Ilyas and went to Mewat as well to obtain a firsthand knowledge of the work. Among them were some teachers of Nadwatul Ulema, Lucknow, and when, on their return, they related their experiences, it came as a pleasant surprise to many. Some of them even called it a 'discovery' and were surprised how a thing like that could remain in obscurity for such a long time.

The Maulana welcomed the visitors with open arms whose number grew with the passage of time. Interest in the aims and efforts of the Tablighi jama'at was no longer confined to Mewat.

Plan of work in Delhi

The Maulana made Hafiz Maqbool Hasan the Amir of all the Tabligh Jama'ats of Delhi, due to whose keenness and the sincere devotion of Hafiz Fakhruddin, more method and coordination was brought about in the functioning of the Jama'ats.

It was arranged that the Tabligh workers stayed at Nizamuddin on every Friday night, and all the Jama'ats assembled in the Jam'a Masjid on the last Wednesday of each month for mutual consultation. The Maulana made it a point to be present at the monthly gatherings at Jam'a Masjid and wanted the Ulema, also, to come. Whoever spent a few Frida nights at Nizamuddin became inclined towards the Movement. Often, they all would dine together. Before and after the meal, the Maulana would speak on the subject that was so dear to his heart. Sometimes, he spoke with great fervour, and, sometimes, with such absorption that the sense of time was lost and the Isha service had to be delayed. Once, the clock struck twelve while it was being celebrated. After the Fajr prayers, the Maulana would, again, address the gathering or ask someone else to speak on his behalf. Some persons who had not stayed for the night, too, participated in the morning service. Respectable people from New Delhi and modern-educated Muslims and teachers of Jamia Millia, including Dr. Zakir Husain[1], would, often, join the Fajr service and return after the Maulana's speech.

Merchants of Delhi

The businessmen of Delhi, generally, were attached to the Maulana. The elderly people among them had been coming to Nizamuddin from the time of Maulana Mohammad Ismail and Maulana Mohammad. After the Mewatis, it was the merchants of Delhi who held the Maulana in the highest esteem. They visited Nizamuddin regularly, particularly on Friday nights, often spending the whole night there. When an important meeting was held in Mewat, they went to attend it in hired buses, taking food with them which was prepared in Delhi, and did the rounds of the neighbouring villages with the *Tabligh* Jama'ats of the Mewatis.

The Maulana, also, attended the various functions at their houses and took advantage of such occasions to deliver his message.

[1] Later the President of the Republic of India.

He treated their children as his own, sharing with them their joys and sorrows, and finding ways of making them interested in his life's mission. With the elders, especially the friends of his father and brother, the Maulana behaved with utmost respect, yet he took them to task if they neglected the *Tabligh* work, and they, too, bore his indignation cheerfully.

Owing to regular contact with the Maulana and as a result of going out on *Tabligh* tours along with the Ulema and other men of faith, the traders of Delhi gained in religious awareness and a welcome change was noticed in their social and moral conduct and monetary dealings. As a rule, the Maulana did not touch upon the details. His method was to produce a general inclination for faith which, in due course, led to the realisation of its worth and significance and engendering of respect for the commands of the Shariat. By and by, the businessmen who did not like to employ bearded men at their shops began to grow a beard themselves and those who thought that an employee who observed Namaz regularly would be a liability as a good deal of his working time would be taken up by it, started going out on *Tabligh* rounds during the busiest hours. They, now, felt no disgrace in walking on foot or moving about in the marketplaces with their luggage on their backs or sleeping on the floor or pressing the bodies of their companions or cooking the meals. In short, with the change in the environment, lives of thousands of men were transformed.

Monetary assistance

Impressed by the growing popularity of the Movement and seeing the huge expenditure it entailed, the merchants and other benevolent and well-meaning people of Delhi and some other places came up with offers of monetary aid. But the Maulana had a fixed principle about it. He did not consider the donation of money as a substitute for active participation and plainly told such people that he needed them and not their wealth. He accepted monetary help only from those who took an active part in the *Tabligh* endeavour. During the most glorious days of Islam, too, that was the general principle, and we find that the names of those who spent freely in the cause of faith, also, occur on the top of the list of the truthful Believers who were, actually, in the forefront of the struggle.

Anyhow, the Maulana willingly accepted money from those who joined hands with him in the *Tabligh* work and in whose sincerity he had a full faith. Notable among them were Haji Nasim Button-Waley (of Sadar Bazar, Delhi) and Mohammad Shafi Quraishi.

Meetings

Generally, a public meeting was held every month at some place in Mewat, and, once in a year, in the Madrassa of Nooh in which, apart from the *Tabligh Jama'ats*, the Muslim traders of Delhi and those who were staying at Nizamuddin, and some Ulema and teachers of Mazaahirul Uloom, Nadwatul Ulema and the Madrassa of Fatehpur, also, participated. The Maulana came with a party of co-workers, preaching his massage all the way. Fellow- travellers in the bus or railway compartment who, generally, used to be associated, in various ways, with the Movement, profited by the discourse, and, thus, as one would say, it was a mobile conference which started with the commencement of the journey from Nizamuddin.

On hearing of the Maulana's arrival, people of the town or village in which the meeting was to be held came out in large numbers to greet him. The Maulana would shake hands with them, seated in the conveyance, and then, he was taken into the town amidst scenes of affection and enthusiasm.

During the days of the conference, the Maulana lived mostly among the poor Mewatis and rested for the night in the mosque. He felt refreshed and reinvigorated as soon as he reached Mewat, and streams of religious knowledge and transcendental truths seemed to flow from him. It was only rarely that the Maulana took rest while in Mewat.

A unique religious and spiritual atmosphere used to pervade the whole place on such occasions. The mosques overflowed with devotees and reverberated with Zikr. Rows of the worshippers had to be formed on the streets. The spectacle at the last quarter of the night was, particularly, heart-lifting. Hardy Mewatis were seen lying in cold, wintry nights in the courtyards of the mosques or under a tree, covered only with a cotton sheet or blanket. When it rained in winter, they would sit patiently of blanket. When it rained in winter, they would sit patiently under leaking Shamianas[1] or dripping trees and listen for hours to the speeches of the Ulema.

Discourses and sermons constituted only a subsidiary part of the congregations. The real emphasis was on forming new *Jama'ats* and sending them out. The success of a meeting was assessed in terms of *Jama'ats* offering to go out of their region. How many people denoted how much time? That was the question. It was the Maulana's sole demand. He asked for no other favour, and, personally, supervised over the work of the conferences from that point of view. Aside of it, experienced Mewatis and the *Moballighin*[2]

---

[1] Meaning a canopy.

[2] Preachers.

of Nizamuddin worked among the headmen of the biradris[1] and other prominent people and theologists to enlist their support in the formation for *Jama'ats.*

There was no peace for the Maulana until he had obtained satisfaction that some solid work had been done Without it, it was very difficult for him to return to Nizamuddin, but once he was assured that progress had been made, no entreaty or consideration of comfort could make him delay his departure by a day or even a few hours.

Sometimes, the Mewatis and Moballighin of Nizamuddin would go in advance to prepare the ground for the meeting. They sought to produce the inclination and ability among the masses to profit from the preachers and the Ulema, and, often, stayed back after the conference to familiarise the new-comers with the aims and principles of the Movement and guide their willingness along the right lines.

Many Mewatis would do bait at the Maulana's hand during his stay. While taking the bait the Maulana would speak at length on *Tabligh*, and take from them the pledge to work for the cause.

At Nooh

A magnificent conference was held at Nooh, in Gurgaon, on the 28th 29th and 30th of November, 1941. Such a large gathering had, at no time, been seen in Mewat. About 25,000 persons attended

[1] A body of persons belonging to the same caste or in the same business or profession.

the meeting, many of whom had covered the distance of 40 or 50 miles on foot, carrying their provisions on their shoulders.

Maulana Husain Ahmad Madani led the Friday congregation under the spacious Shamiana of the Conference, and the service was, also, held in the Jam'a Masjid and in all the other mosques of the town, but so large was the concourse that people were seen offering the prayers on the house-tops and in the streets.

The Conference began after the Friday service, and, for the next two days, it continued to be in session, with brief intervals, from the morning till the evening. There was no Chairman, no Reception Committee and no Volunteer Corps, and yet the whole event went off in a most orderly and dignified manner.

Giving his impressions of the meeting, Mufti Kifayatullah[1] said: "I have been attending different political and religious conferences for the last 35 years, but I have yet to see a more impressive gathering."

In addition to the regular sessions, the Maulana spoke after each prayer-service as well.

Expansion

Parties of Mewatis and merchants of Delhi and students of the Madrassas began to visit U.P., and the Punjab, and tours were undertaken of Khurja, Aligarh, Agra, Bulandshahr, Meerut Panipat, Sonepat, Karnal, and Rohtak. At some of these places, Tabligh

---

[1] Mufti Kifaytullah was the greatest Alum (theologian) and Mufti (legist) of India of his time. He was the President of Jami'at Ulema-i-Hind for many years.

Jama'ats, also, were formed and people came regularly from there to Nizamuddin.

At the request of Haji Abdul Jabbar and Haji Abdus Sattar, a Jama'at went to Karachi in February 1943, and another in April of the same years under the leadership of Syed Raza Husain.

The Maulana wanted the Movement to spread along the Western coast in the hope that from there it might reach the coastline of Arabia, and then, penetrate into the hinterland. Many Arabs and other West Asian Muslims lived in the port towns of Bombay and Karachi, and the Maulana thought that if the Movement became popular among them, they might take it back to their countries.

Trip to Lucknow

The teachers and pupils of Nadwatul Ulema had been working along the Maulana's lines, since 1940, in the Suburbs of Lucknow, and also visiting Nizamuddin regularly during the vacations etc... The Maulana, too, had developed a liking for the Jama'at of Nadwa.

In 1943, the Maulana agreed to come to Lucknow. Before him, a party of about 40 Mewatis and traders of Delhi arrived in order to prepare the ground for the visit.

Every day, the party used to leave Nadwa after the Asr prayers for doing the rounds of a few *mohallas*, which included speeches on the aims, and principles of the *Tabligh* movement. It returned after 10 o'clock in the night.

In the morning, after the Fajr service, the members of the *Jama'at* would meet for study and instruction which formed an important part of the *Tabligh* tour. A part of time was devoted to the correction of the sound and accent in the recitation of the Quran, a part of it to learning about the rules and principles of the Shariat, and a part to the narration of events from the lives of the holy Companions and stories of Jehad. Lastly, they were taught the principles and methods of *Tabligh* which included practical training. The mid-day meal was, then, served, and, after a little rest, the *Jama'at* would go out to fulfil its evening routine after the Asr prayers.

On July 18, the Maulana arrived with Hafiz Fakhruddin, Maulana Ihtishamul Hasan, Mohammad Shafi Quraishi, and Haji Nasim. On his way from Railway Station to Nadwa, he offered *Nafl* prayers on the grassy plot near the Moti Mahal Bridge and supplicated to the Lord for a long time. At Nadwa, the Maulana, first of all, went to the mosque where the *Jama'ats* were sitting in groups and receiving instructions from their leaders. In spite of intense desire and devotion, no one rose from his place to greet the Maulana. The Maulana cast an affectionate glance on all of them and shook hands with the Amir, Hafiz Maqbool Hasan.

Maulana Syed Sulaiman Nadwi had come a day earlier, and, on the next day, Sheikhul Hadees Maulana Mohammad Zakaria, Maulana Mohammad Manzoor Nomani, Maulana Abdul Haq Madani and some teachers of Mazaahirul Uloom, also, arrived.

Besides formal gatherings in various parts of the town, the Maulana spoke about his mission to the visitors who came to see him daily in large numbers. He hardly missed an opportunity to propagate the cause to which he had dedicated his life. He, also, called on Maulana Abdul Shakoor Farooqi and Maulana Qutub Mian Firangi Mahli and went to Idara-i-Talimat-i-Islam.

The last day of his stay, which happened to be a Friday, was a day of exceptional activity. In the morning, the Maulana attended a function of Jami'atul Isla, which was the name of the Students' Union of Nadwa, and then, visited the Amiruddaula Islamia College, where a large crowd had gathered to receive him. He offered the Friday prayers at the mosque of Mamoon Bhanjey ki Qabr. After the service was over, the Maulana made a fervent appeal to the people to go to Kanpur with the Jama'at from Delhi, but there was no response. It hurt him very much, and in a highly agitated state, he went and shut the gate of the mosque and posted guards at it, and standing under the middle arch, he began to exhort the people. He asked some of them to stand up and tell what excuse they had to offer. If they could travel for a worldly need, why could they not do so for the sake of faith? What was there to prevent them from setting out in the path of God? Addressing Haji Wali Mohammad, who had been ill for some time, the Maulana said, "why do you not go?" "I am dying", he replied. "If you must die," retorted the Maulana, "Go and die in Kanpur," At last, Haji Wali Mohammad agreed and the journey was accomplished by him safely. Eight or ten persons, also, went along with him, some of whom proved very useful for the cause.

The Maulana left for Rae Bareli the night train, reaching *Takia*[1] at about 3 a.m.

---

[1] A small settlement, on the bank of the river Sai, in Rae Bareli. It was founded by Shah Alamullah Naqshbandi and has the distinction of being the home of Syed Ahmad Shaheed.

Chapter VI:
Journey's end

The health of Maulana Mohammad Ilyas had never been good, Ceaseless work and worry, constant travelling, irregular hours and complete disregard of medical advice could only aggravate the abdominal complaint that had been his constant companion since childhood. In November 1943, he had a severe attack of dysentery from which he was never to recover. Whoever came from Delhi in those days brought the news that the Maulana's illness was continuing; he was growing weaker day by day, and yet there was no relaxation in his efforts. If anything, his fervour had increased. As a friend, Abdul Jabbar Saheb of Gonda, wrote from Delhi, in January 1944.

> "By the grace of God, the Maulana is improving, but he is, still, very weak. He insists on talking against the advice of his physicians. He says that he would prefer to die from talking for the sake of *Tabligh* than regaining health by observing silence. In his view. The real cause of his illness was the indifference of the Ulema towards the *Tabligh* work. They should come forward because they possessed the knowledge and understanding of faith. If they had to borrow money for it, they should not worry. God will grant an increase in their sustenance. His illness. was a blessing. People ought to come, at least, on hearing of it, but they don't. He was seeing a clear proof of the propitiousness of his illness. While the Maulana was saying it, especially the last sentence, his condition was such that I have no words to describe it."

In the same month, a *Jama'at* including Maulana Hafiz Imran Khan of Nadwa and Hakim Qasim Husain went from Lucknow to Delhi. The Maulana had become very weak, but he could, still, walk unaided and lead the prayer- services. He, however, needed support to get up from his seat. The disease had advanced considerably, and it was apparent that the end was not far away. Mirwaiz Maulana Mohammad Yusuf of Kashmir was staying at Nizamuddin at that time, and when the party from Lucknow arrived, it found the Maulana explaining to him why it was essential for the Ulema to take an active part in the *Tabligh* movement. It was the main worry of the Maulana during those days and the sole topic of his conversation. He strongly felt that men who could know and understand remained with him, listening to what he said and acquiring a full understanding of the rules and principles of the Movement. He wanted to impress upon the Ulema that the *Tabligh* call was only worthy of them, and they, alone, were worthy of it. It could prosper simply when they took it up. His own similitude was that of a man who saw a house on fire and called out to people to come and put it out. His duty was to warn; it was for others to extinguish the fire.

The Maulana urged upon the Delhi merchants and *Moballighin* the need to enlist the services of the Ulema. A number of meetings were organised for that purpose which were addressed by distinguished theologists like Mufti Kifayatullah, Maulana Abdul Hannan, and Maulana Imran Khan.

The Maulana waited eagerly for the report of these meetings and would not go to bed until he had received a firsthand account from different persons. Sometimes, people returned late from the meetings, but there was no sleep for the Maulana till he had talked to them.

The Maulana, generally, spoke after breakfast and dinner which would, often, go on for hours and leave him thoroughly exhausted.

Contact with the Ulema

A major objective of the Maulana's endeavour was to build bridges between the different groups and classes of Muslims and to rekindle the sentiments of trust and goodwill among them so that they could co-operate with one another in the service of Islam. He did not want to ignore even the religiously backward sections and considered the mutual quarrels and prejudices of the Muslims a grievous misfortune of the Millet and a danger to the future of Islam. The Maulana believed that through the *Tabligh* movement it would be possible to bring the Ulema and the common people close to each other, encouraging signs of which had already begun to appear.

While addressing a meeting of the Ulema at Ghat Mika, in compliance with Maulana Mohammad Yousuf's orders, I had tried to emphasise that if the Ulema did not improve their contacts with the Muslim masses through *Tabligh* movement, they would get isolated in the community. The Maulana showed much pleasure when Maulana Mohammad Yusuf gave a summary of the speech to him.

The Maulana, on the one hand, asked the Ulema to feel sympathetically for the masses and keep directly in touch with them, and, on the other, exhorted the masses to show proper respect to them and visit them regularly. To the *Tabligh* workers, he taught the ways of associating the Ulema with the Movement. He sent them to spend some time with the Ulema, and, on their return, enquired from them in detail about what they had seen and felt. If they expressed any criticism, the Maulana would correct them.

The Maulana, thus, brought a rapport between the Ulema and the common people the like of which had, probably, not been seen since the Khilafat agitation.

Rapprochement

A great deal of animosity and mistrust existed among the various groups of Ahl-i-Sunnat, which stemmed mostly from differences over minor issues and had been accentuated by the practice of living in water-tight compartments. Every group sought security in keeping itself to itself and shutting its eyes to what was good in the others.

Dialectical combats and polemical disputations had been supposed to be the most suitable means of resolving the differences, but, as experience had shown, these exercise only lent fuel to the fire. What the Maulana wanted was that knots of the minds were loosened through politeness and good understanding, and by personal contact. Once the different groups came to know each other more intimately, the suspicions and misgivings among them would disappear. By working together in the cause of faith in a constructive way and along the right lines, the differences would lose their intensity, and it would be possible to keep them within reasonable limits.

Advanced stage of illness

By March 1944, the Maulana's illness had advanced so much that he could no longer lead the prayers-service. He had to take the support of two men to come to attend the service and joined it in the sitting posture. He, often, said it, apparently, was his last illness, though one should not despair of the mercy of the Lord. In those days, the Maulana delivered two memorable speeches in which he indicated that his end was near, but in it, too, there lay a profound design and purpose of the Lord.

Arrival of the Ulema

Maulana Hafiz Hashim Jan Mujaddidi had learned about the *Tabligh* movement from the *Jama'ats* that went to Sind and had formed a very high opinion of Maulana Mohammad Ilyas. He came to Delhi in March, which made the Maulana very happy, and he took a personal interest in the arrangements for his stay. The participation of men of learning and character whose ancestors, also, had rendered a valuable service to Faith was an unfailing source of joy to him. Maulana Hafiz Hashim Jan Mujaddidi being a descendant of Hazrat Mujaddid Alf-Sani, his coming possessed a great significance for the Maulana. A few days later, my elder brother, Dr. Syed Abdul Ali, also, came from Lucknow. The Maulana embraced him while lying in bed, expressed pleasure at his coming and said that it had made him feel better. It was not uncommon for the Maulana to show a sudden improvement in his health when a good and encouraging thing happened in connection with the Movement.

The Maulana wanted to utilise the services of the religious and spiritual leaders in the circles in which they were known, but which had not responded to the call of *Tabligh*. He did not let their visit remain a personal affair, but insisted upon his colleagues to turn it to good account by taking from them the work that was worthy of their high station.

The Maulana told Dr. Syed Abdul Ali to spend some time with the old and experienced Mewatis. He did not like his putting up in the room at the rear of the mosque, and once, remarked that he who resided outside the mosque, should not be considered to have come. Upon it, Dr. Syed Abdul Ali started spending most of his time in the mosque and admitted that he felt a distinct gain in remaining with the Mewatis and the Moballighs.

The teachers and administrators of the Islamic Madrassas met to consider what their institutions could do for the Movement. Among those who took part in the deliberations were Maulana Mohammad Tayyab, Mufti Kifayatullah, Molvi Mohammad Shafi, Maulana Hafiz Abdul Latif, Maulana Aizaz Ali, and Sheikhul Hadees Maulana Mohammad Zakaria.

Third Jama'at to Sind

In the beginning of April, a party of about 60 persons left for Sind under the leadership of Hafiz Maqbool Hasan. It made a brief halt at Lahore where some of its members called on Hazrat Nurul Masha'ikh of Kabul who happened to be there during those days.

Jama'at From Peshawar

Some friends of Peshawar wrote to Maulana Mohammad Ilyas expressing the desire to come to Delhi in April, and, in their letter, they, also, said that the Maulana's life and well-being was "the property of Islam and a most precious possession of the Muslims", and so, the Maulana, too, should pray for his long lie and good health. In his reply, the Maulana, wrote:

> "May Allah bless your arrival in April, but it seems more appropriate that before coming, you worked among your own people for some time in accordance with the rules and

proprieties of the *Tabligh* movement. Your visit will, then, be most beneficial.

"I pray for my health, but with the condition that I am able to spend my time in conformity with the schedule and no part of it is spent purposelessly as the case is now, in my present condition. I should take a hand only in what cannot be done without me, otherwise the *Jama'at* must take the responsibility for everything. I have learnt this lesson from my illness."

After making a few *Tabligh* rounds and doing some field work, a small *Jama'at* consisting of Arshad Saheb, Maulana Ihsanullah, Mistri Abdul Quddus and two children arrived from Peshawer and stayed at Nizamuddin from the 10th to the 14th of April. Arshad Saheb had maintained a daily record of his activities and personal observations from which we can obtain an idea of the life at Nizamuddin. It reads:

"At about 1 o'clock a child brought the news that the meal was ready. The Maulana's room is in a corner of the mosque. We went to it. The meal was laid there, and the Maulana was sitting on a charpoy, supported by pillows and covered with a quilt. His frugal meal, as prescribed by the physician, had been placed before him. His face was luminous while the body had been reduced to a sack of bones. His physician was sitting on the floor, near the charpoy, We sat down to the meal after paying our respects to him. In all, there were twenty to Twenty-five men. During the meal, the Maulana made the following observations:

"(i) Hakim Saheb! I consider it a religious duty to follow your instructions. But does it mean nothing that I am deprived of the Divine reward on Qayam[1] in Namaz?

"(ii) Brothers! God has a special affection for his bondmen, even the infidels. It is this affection that has led to the use of the following words in the Quran. regarding Hazrat Yunus (Jonah): And the fish swallowed him while he was blameworthy. (XXXVII: 142)

"(The) Maulana emphasised the word Maleem, i.e., blameworthy). 'When such is the love of the Lord for the infidels', he said, 'what will it be for the Believers? In the service of the Believers lies the essence of servility. And what is servility? It is to make oneself lowly for the sake of the Believers. This is the cardinal principle of our Movement which no theologist, layman or materialist can refute.' After it, Maulana condemned vanity and hypocrisy, and, with it, the sitting came to an end.

"At the time of Zuhr, the Maulana came out, leaning on a stick and supported by two men, and sat down, resting his back against the pulpit. He said:

(1) Brothers! We have not only deviated but deviated far from the faith of the Prophet. Government or any other form of political power can never be the goal of a Muslim. If we come into power through adherence to the path of the Prophet, we are not going to shirk it. But surely, it is not our aim. We have only to give everything, including our lives, in this path.

---

[1] The posture of standing erect in Namaz.

"'(II) Remember the eradication of the evils rampant among the Muslims does not take place by enumerating them or dwelling upon their evilness. What needs be done is to enlarge and heighten the few virtues that may be present in them. The evils will disappear by themselves.'

"After it, the people stood up for the service and two men helped the Maulana, also, to stand: Strangely enough, a man who could not move from his place without the support of two persons was carrying out Qayam[1], Ruku[2], Sajda[3] and Jalsa[4] perfectly and with ease in all the four Raka'ts of the service.

"When the Namaz was over, the Maulana said:

"Know that you have not come here to sit on the Masnad. Do not allow your time to be wasted. Always remain occupied with Zikr and education. You have come here for a very short time. It is nothing."

"He, then, added with utmost earnestness:

"Bring a larger Jama'at when you come again and stay for a longer period. It is necessary to stay here as long as possible.'

"The Maulana went back to his apartment after the prayer-service, supported by two persons. sons. Those of us who were present were then, divided into two groups, one of the Arabic-knowing people and the other of the non-Arabic- knowing people.

---

[1] The Posture of standing erect.in Namaz.

[2] Bowing low in Namaz.

[3] Bending forward in Namaz with the forehead touching the ground.

[4] The act of seating oneself between the two Sajdas of the same Rak'at.

Instruction was imparted to the non- Arabic-knowing people from the Urdu books relating to the Movement while to the Arabic-knowing people, a few Traditions were read out from Kitab-ul-Iman which was followed by a discussion. I was told that it was essential for everyone staying at Nizamuddin to complete that course of study.

"At night, the Jama'at from Peshawar carried out *Tabligh* in Paharganj, along with other Jama'ats, spending the whole night there.

APRIL 12:

"In the forenoon, we met together for the study of the Traditions. The Maulana was looking better at teatime. He said to me, 'Brother, send a bigger *Jama'at*. Even an ordinary thing cannot be done in the world without acquiring the necessary knowledge, so, much so that a mentor is needed even to become a thief. If you commit theft without proper training, you will be caught. So, how can one become proficient in important things like *Tabligh* without gaining knowledge and skill in it?' Then, gently, he asked, 'Now, brother, will you bring the *Jama'at*? 'If a *Jama'at* first came to Peshawar from here, I replied, 'It would be easier to make the people there interested in *Tabligh*.'

"The Maulana remarked, 'Look. Write yourself and ask the other influential to persons of Peshawar, also, to write to them to bring the Jama'at. The Jama'at will, then, come to your town and these people who have so far been sitting on the Masnad, too, will become active.'

"After Zuhr, the Maulana busied himself with the formation of Jama'ats and giving them necessary instructions before departure.

"In the afternoon, we had another round of the Traditions, and Maulana Wasif read out some wonderful reports from Kitah-ul-Jehad.

"A large number of persons have come in connection with the Fair and Urs[1] (of Hazrat Nizamuddin Auliya) and *Tabligh* is being done among them.

APRIL 13:

"At tea-time, the Maulana said that 'like the earlier Prophets, our Prophet, too, brought the Shariat. The Bible of Jesus Christ has not revoked the Torah, but only made alterations in its commands, while the Quran of the holy Prophet has repealed all the former scriptures, and it is, now, forbidden to follow them directly.

"It was the method of *Tabligh* that distinguished our Prophet from the other Prophets. As the chain of Apostleship had continued after the earlier Apostles, they did not pay as much attention to it as the Prophet Mohammad, for the Order of Apostles was to cease after him, and the entire responsibility of *Tabligh* had to be borne by his followers.'

"The Maulana, then, shed light on the doctrine of 'There is no loyalty to the creatures in the transgression of the law of the Creator,' and observed that it should, permanently, be kept

[1] Anniversary of a Sufi-saint.

in the mind in worldly affairs, even in one's attitude towards parents, teachers or spiritual mentors.

"Addressing Maulana Ihsanullah, the Maulana said, did you follow, Molvi Sahib. This work is the jewel of the earliest times. Sacrifice everything, even your life, for it. The greater the sacrifice you make, the more will be your gain.

"You are listening to it and enjoying it. But it is like the joy one feels on seeing the fruit in other people's orchards. The real joy lies in growing the fruit in your own orchard, and how can it be done without toil and sacrifice!'

"It began to rain heavily at the time of Asr. The *Tabligh* was suspended for the day. When Maulana came for the Asr prayers, he was angry to know that the Jama'at had not gone out on the daily round. He spoke of the faith and sacrifices of Mewatis and remarked that these people are your benefactors. They have shown you the correct path.' He, then, called a Mewati and telling him to sit by him, observed, 'When I, first, told him to go and do the *Tabligh*, he asked what was Tablid. (He was so ignorant that he could not even pronounce the word *Tabligh* correctly). I, thereupon, told him to teach the Kalima to the people Mo which he, again, replied that he did not know it. I, then, said to him to go and tell the people that though he had grown old, he did not know the Kalima. So, they must go to someone and learn it.'

"Stirred by the Maulana's speech, the *Jama'ats* set out, after Asr, in the rain. Glory be! It stopped raining as soon as the party had started and the weather became pleasant. The programme of *Tabligh* was carried out in a village about half-a-mile away and the party returned after Maghrib.

"On Thursday, many prominent persons came from Delhi to pay their respects to the Maulana. Thus, today, there is a very good gathering, in spite of the rain, and it has been my good fortune to see so many blessed faces.

APRIL 14:

"I found most of the people engaged in Zikr and Tahlil[1] after Tahajjud[2]. Our friend, Maulana Ihsanullah led the Fajr Service at the order of the Maulana. Over fifty persons were present at breakfast.

The Maulana said:

"(i) The reward on the recital of a small Sura of the Quran Sura-i-Fateha in Namaz is greater than on the recital of the whole the Quran outside of it. From it, one can imagine the reward earned by the Jama'at, which exhorts the people to observe Namaz. An act reveals its special quality at a particular time and occasion. Thus, Zikr during Jehad fetches a much greater reward than at home or in a hospice. So, friends, do the Zikr much and often.

"(ii) What is this Movement? To act upon: Go forth, light-armed and heavy-armed. (IX: 41). Negligence in this going forth amounts to calling upon oneself the Wrath of God. It is essential to observe the rules and principle in the work of *Tabligh*. If any rule or principle is disregarded, the punishment of the Lord, which might, otherwise, have been delayed, will visit you at once. On two occasions, in the past, the Movement has suffered a severe setback, owing to the neglect of the rules,

---

[1] Act of repeating the Kalima of Laa ilaaha- il- lallah.

[2] A special Namaz offered during the later part of the night.

when, apparently, it was at the peak. So, brothers, follow strictly the six fundamental principles.

"(iii) What is Islam? To bow one's head before the Command that is for the existing time. The Devil dissuades us from it. He misleads us in two ways: by making the evil deeds look attractive, and, thus, inciting our carnal self to indulge in them, and by persuading us to give up a superior act for an inferior one. He induces us to perform a supererogatory deed when an obligatory duty has to be observed and leads us to believe that we are doing a virtuous thing. The most important task, at the present time, is *Tabligh* and not even the highest act of worship can take its place.'

"At tea-time, it was decided that the Jama'at from Peshawar would leave for Saharanpur the next morning for *Tabligh* along with a Jama'at of Delhi. We went to the Maulana for leave-taking. The Maulana enquired why we had not brought the children with us upon which we offered an excuse. He remarked, "You do not take care of the instruction and training of the children and take shelter behind their simplicity. It is not necessary that the children understood a thing. What is needed, simply, is to put it into their ears, to show it to them, and to make them conscious of it. Or else, what does the saying of Azan in the ears of a newly born child mean?

"The Maulana, then, exhorted us to carry out Zikr habitually and frequently. He said, 'Zikr is like an impregnable fortress in order that the Devil does not. attack and overpower you. In the remembrance of Allah do hearts find rest.

Moreover, brothers, teach good and virtuous things to your children.'

"At saharanpur, Molvi Abdul Ghaffar Nadwi met us. He had come after meeting the Maulana at Delhi and brought the following message from him: 'You came and are going back after sitting on the Masnad for a few days. Remember, you have to undergo hunger and thirst in the path of God. Shed your sweat in this path and be ready to shed your blood also.'"

Total Absorption

We proceed to reproduce a few incidents related by Maulana Mohammad Manzoor Nomani in order to show how overpowering was the Maulana's anxiety for *Tabligh* even when he was critically ill. Writes Maulana Nomani:

"Maulana Syed Ataullah Shah Bukhari came to visit Maulana Mohammad Ilyas in the last week of April. Two days earlier, the Maulana had suffered a severe attack which had left him so weak that he could hardly talk for two or three minutes continuously On hearing of the arrival of Shah Sahib, he summoned me and said, 'I have some important things to discuss with Maulana Ataullah Shah Bukhari and the manner of it will be that you will keep your ear close to my mouth and listen attentively, and, then, tell him what I say'. Thus, when Shah Saheb was called in, the Maulana began the conversation with him through me, but after a few minutes, he regained enough strength to speak to him directly, and went on talking continually for about half-an-hour.

"The day on which the Maulana had the attack, he remained unconscious for nearly two hours. Then, suddenly, he opened the eyes, and said: Truth is high; Truth in high; It is not made High. After it, in a state of ecstasy, he recited the following verse thrice in a slightly melodious voice, which was rather unusual with him: To help the believers is incumbent upon us. (XXX:47)

"I was in the courtyard of the mosque when the Maulana recited the verse. On hearing it, I went and stood at the door of his room. At the same time, the Maulana enquired about me; so, I went in: The Maulana said to me, 'Molvi Saheb! It is the promise of Allah that this work will be done, and by His Help, it will be carried to completion. But it is essential that, with utmost faith in His promise, you sought His Help, and strove as hard as you could, and did not slacken your efforts."

"He, then, again, closed his eyes and remained silent for some time, after which he remarked, 'would to God that the Ulema took charge of the Movement and I departed (from the world).' "Strangely enough, the Maulana's solicitude for the revival of Faith increased as his condition worsened. For months he lingered in a state of exhaustion in which people do not even like to be spoken to, but during all that time, the Maulana was found either deeply concerned with the progress of the Movement or beseeching the Lord to grant sincerity and steadfastness to those who were associated with it. The limit was that he would, first, talk to his physicians about him mission and only then allow them to examine. Once, when Mufti Kifayatullah brought a leading doctor of Delhi to treat him, he spoke to him thus:

"Doctor Saheb! You possess an art and people derive benefit from it. But it is an art to throw which into the shade, Jesus was sent down with some manifest miracles like healing the blind and reviving the dead, but this much you will appreciate that the inner knowledge that was vouchsafed to him was very much superior to the miracles. Now, what I want to tell you is that the spiritual truths and commandments that were revealed to our Prophet, the Last of the Divine Apostles, Peace and Blessings of the Lord be on him, repealed and abrogated the spiritual truths and commandments sent down through Jesus. So, imagine the worth of what a great thing do we fail to appreciate when we neglect the transcendental truth revealed by the sacred Prophet. We tell the people to avail themselves of this bounty of the Lord, otherwise they will be in a great loss."

"The Maulana was not willing to speak about or listen to anything aside of his favourite theme of regeneration of Islam. Often, he would promptly check anyone who began to talk of some other thing in his presence. If an attendant enquired about his health, he said, 'Brother, illness and health are a part of life. What is 'welfare' or 'none-welfare' in it? Welfare means that the task for which we have been born is done, and the soul of the blessed Prophet rests in peace. Even a minor alteration in the state in which the Prophet had left the Companions was considered by them to be contrary to welfare.'"

Haji Abdul Rahman relates that some relatives of the Maulana came from Kandhla to see him. "What brings you here?"

the Maulana asked. "To enquire about your welfare," they replied. "You come from Kandhla", said the Maulana, "to enquire about his welfare who has been born to perish and care nothing for the Prophet's Faith which was meant to be eternal, but is dying."

On a Friday, Maulana Mohammad Yusuf led the Fajr service in which he recited Qunoot-i-Naazila. After the prayers, an attendant informed Maulana Mohammad Yusuf that Maulana Mohammad Ilyas wanted to see him, and when he went to the Maulana, the Maulana said to him, "In Qunoot-i-Naazila, formulate the intention with regard to the non-Muslim religious mendicants and hermits, also, along with the Infidels, who are employing the power of their hearts in opposition to Faith." He, then, recalled how in a polemical contest at Saharanpur a Hindu hermit was directing his psychic strength against the Muslim disputant and the Muslims disputant was having difficulty in expressing his ideas. Maulana Khalil Ahmad, also, was present at the contest. When his attention was drawn to it and he concentrated, the hermit got scared and left the meeting in haste. After it, the Muslim disputant began to speak freely."

It was customary for the Maulana to address the gathering on Friday nights when people came not only from the different localities of Delhi, but, also, from other towns. During the Maulana's illness, the number of visitors grew even more. The Maulana could not speak himself, but he could not, also, allow the time of those who took pains to come to Nizamuddin solely for the sake of Faith to be wasted and their visit to become a personal affair which ended with anxious inquiries about his health etc.

On a Friday night, people were told to collect on the roof of the mosque, and it was assigned to me to address them. The start was delayed by few minutes during which the Maulana sent the message thrice to hasten as every minute was telling upon his nerves.

Last month

The Maulana's condition was deteriorating day by day. It being no longer possible for him to offer up Namaz standing, his cot was placed at the end of the row to enable him to join the service.

In those days, Maulana Zafar Ahmad was looking after the Maulana's needs. Sheikhul Hadees Maulana Mohammad Zakaria, also, came on June 21. A few days later, the annual meeting of Madrassa-i-Moinul Islam of Nooh was to be held which, perhaps, was going to be the first meeting without the Maulana. The party from Nizamuddin left for Nooh in a lorry on the morning of June 23, under the leadership of Maulana Mohammad Yusuf. The journey was taken up with Zikr and religious discourses, and the meeting began soon after its arrival at 2 p.m. The garden laid by the Maulana was spread on all sides, and it was in full bloom. Only the gardener was not there.

As the evening session was in progress, the boarding house of the English High School of Nooh caught fire. When, on our return, the incident was mentioned to him, he remarked, "You slackened in Zikr and the Devil had his opportunity." As it was an English School, one of us showed pleasure at the destruction of its building, and though the Maulana remained quiet at that time, the expression of joy at the loss of anything associated with the Muslims hurt him deeply, and, on a suitable occasion, he made known his feelings and said that it was no laughing matter.

The Maulana enquired from Maulana Mohammad Yusuf if he had shown the spectacle of the departure of the *Jama'ats* to Maulana Zafar Ahmad and when he replied in the negative, the Maulana remarked that he should have done so as it gave an idea of how the deputations of Muslims went out during the days of the Prophet.

As the hour of death approached

The Maulana know well that death was near. Sometimes, he would give expression to it in order to infuse a sense of urgency among the colleagues. When Maulana Zafar Ahmad came to see him, he said, "You promised to lend me your time, but you have not done so." As Maulana Zafar Ahmad replied that it was too hot and he would come in the Ramzan vacations and spend some time with him, the Maulana remarked, "You are talking of Ramzan and I do not hope to be alive even in Sh'aban[1]."

One day, the Maulana told Chowdhri Nawaz Khan not to go. "It is now only a matter of twenty days, a little more or less," he said. The Maulana passed away exactly on the twentieth day.

He had told me many times that he had no hope of recovery, though God had control over all things, and He could, of course, bring him back to health if he liked; Occasionally however, he would, also, say something that revived the hopes of the attendants and made them cheerful.

---

[1] The month preceding Ramzan according to the Islamic calendar.

From the beginning, the Maulana had been under the treatment of Hakim Karim Bakhsh of Paharaganj. Later, he was put under Biochemic treatment on the advice of Maulana Zafar Ahmad. In the end, Dr. Abul Latif, a leading allopath of Delhi was called in. Dr. Shaukatullah Ansari had declared quite early that the Maulana was suffering from abdominal tuberculosis, which, in those days, was considered incurable, but Dr. Abdul Latif disagreed and diagnosed the ailment as chronic dysentery and since it was, comparatively, a less serious condition, it was decided to give him a chance, but there was no improvement in Maulana's health.

Displeasure at mere personal attention

The Maulana was displeased when he felt about anyone that he was attached only to him and not to the cause. Once a Mewati was messaging his head. On recognising him, the Maulana said angrily, "You never take part in *Tabligh*. I am not going to take any service from you. Leave me." In the same way, about and aged gentleman who seemed to be very earnest in caring for him, he said to Maulana Mohammad Manzoor Nomani, "He has a great affection for me, but he does not accept what I have to offer. He has not responded to the call of *Tabligh*. You take him aside and tell him to associate himself actively with the Movement. Without it, it is very painful for me to let him look after my comfort." Maulana Manzoor Nomani, thereupon, spoke to him to which he replied, "I have come, now, with the firm intention of joining the *Tabligh* movement." The Maulana felt highly pleased when Maulana Mohammad Manzoor Nomani reported it back to him and kissed the hands of the old gentleman.

New areas

Letters coming from outside Delhi and Mewat showed that the Movement was making a remarkable progress in those areas. Much enthusiasm was being witnessed and facilities had, unexpectedly, been created in towns which, till then, had presented a gloomy picture. A large *Jama'at* went to Bhopal at the request of Molvi Abdur Rasheed Miskeen while two *Jama'ats* went to Jaipur at the request of Molvi Abdur Rasheed Nomani and Prof. Abdul Mughni. In the forefront of the new regions of expansion was Moradabad from where most encouraging reports came.

The Maulana lay dying, but his enthusiasm for work was undiminished. The nearer the appointed hour approached, the greater did his fervour for *Tabligh* grow. He, personally, supervised the activities at Nizamuddin from the sick-bed and issued instructions at all hours of the day and night.

So sensitive had he grown that anything that was not directly related to his life's mission irked him. Once, during a session of study and instruction, we began to discuss some historical facts and criticism was expressed of Muslim Kings. Somehow, the word of it reached the Maulana who, at once, sent the message through Molvi Moinullah that the topic was to be changed.

About public speeches, the Maulana's standing orders were to keep them short and to the point. The emotional state of the speaker should be the same as used to be of the sacred Prophet while delivering a sermon. (It is related that when the Apostle of God gave a sermon it appeared from his condition that he was giving the warning that the enemy was advancing, and an attack was imminent). The Maulana did not like the speeches to be embellished with anecdotes or verses. He felt uneasy when a speaker began to indulge in rhetoric or seemed to be carried away by force of his eloquence and told him curtly to come down to the main subject or stop speaking.

On a Friday morning there was a large gathering, and I was told to address it. I began in the traditional style of an orator, which was too much for the Maulana, and soon, the word was sent to me not to digress from the subject. The Maulana's cot was taken back to his apartment, and I finished the speech after stating barely what was to be said.

At Asr, the congregation used to be fairly large, and the Maulana's message was read to it. On that Friday, the Maulana could not give a message as he was in a state of Coma. I had learnt the lesson in the morning so when Maulana Mohammad Zakaria told me to speak, I replied, "what can I do? Speech-making will be out of place, and I have nothing to say." When the Maulana regained consciousness, he enquired why the time had been wasted and no speech was delivered. "You had not given any instructions about it," he was told. "Why was I not asked?" he said. On being informed that he was running high fever, and it was decided not to give him trouble in that condition, he observed, "Why did you attach greater importance to my convenience than to the interest of Faith?"

Exceptional care and solicitude

Among the things on which the Maulana was laying greatest stress, in those days, were Zikr and Ilm (the seeking of knowledge). What he feared was that the *Tabligh* mission degenerated into a materialistic effort and a soulless collection of rules and regulations like the other contemporary movements. He said that Zikr and Ilm were the two wheels of the *Tabligh* movement. Knowledge was necessary for Zikr, and Zikr was necessary for knowledge. Without Zikr, knowledge was mere darkness, and without knowledge, Zikr was pure mischief, and the *Tabligh* movement without either was downright materialism.

Secondly, there was the love for the illiterate and downtrodden sections of the Muslims and an earnest anxiety for their religious reform. He established for them a Maktab[1] by the roadside, near the mosque, and another a little farther, near the crossing, where he, also, made the arrangement for drinking water and hookah[2]. The *Moballighs* of Delhi and Mewat were instructed to go and sit there and invite the Muslim passers-by politely and with affection, entertain them with hookah and water and ask them to recite the Kalima and try to promote in them the desire to gain the knowledge of Faith. The Maulana kept himself closely in touch with the affairs of those Maktabs. The *Urs* of Hazrat Khwaja Moinuddin Chishti was being held at Ajmer at that time, and a large number of poor Muslims used to come to the tomb of Nizamuddin Auliya from the neighbouring districts.

---

[1] One need not be misled by the term 'Maktab', There was nothing of the traditional Maktabs or Madrassas about them. Only a coarse carpet was spread on the ground, under a large tree, and a group of *Tabligh* workers were engaged in study and instruction in the manner of Ahl-i- Suffa during the lifetime of the Prophet. It was, also, a part of their duty to establish a rapport with the wayfarers through hookah and drinking-water and bring them into a receptive frame of mind. This was the main idea behind the establishment of the wayside Maktabs.

[2] A Hubble bubble.

When, on the way, they saw the inviting shade of the trees and the provision for hookah and fresh water, they sat down to rest for a while. This gave the *Moballighs* their chance and they took a full advantage of it.

Hundreds of uneducated Muslims were, thus, made familiar with the principal tenets of Islam, and the open-air Maktabs became a source of guidance to them in a natural, effortless manner. Sometimes, the Maulana would send the Ulema, before the Fajr service, to the Mathura Road to carry out *Tabligh* among the Cartmen and camel drivers.

The teaching of the correct way and proprieties of the payment of Zakat was another thing that mattered most with the Maulana during the last days of his life. Merchants and other well-to-do persons, then, used to be with him all the time, and he took the opportunity to stress, again and again, and had it explained, also, by others that a persons should fulfil the duty of Zakat with the same care and attention as was demanded by an act of worship. He ought to seek out the deserving parties himself and pay the Zakat to them with a feeling of gratitude.

Fourthly, the Maulana had grown very particular about his mail. He insisted that the *Tabligh* letters should be read out every morning, after the Fajr Prayers, to those present and their advice sought. Before the presentation of the mail, it was explained that the letters were being placed before them so that they might reflect on the issues contained in them and cultivate the habit of bestowing thought on religious affairs and make a beginning towards employing their mental faculties, which till then were spent only on worldly matters, for the promotion of the aims and objects of Faith. The letters were, generally, about things regarding which the workers of Mewat and Delhi needed advice and the replies were sent through mutual consultation. The Maulana, thus, was preparing the colleagues or the responsibility that was going to fall on their shoulders after his death.

Visitors

The number of visitors was increasing every day. Two to three hundred persons used to be present at all hours of day and night at Nizamuddin, who took their meals, and, also, slept there. No place in the mosque and the boarding house was left unoccupied. There was an air of activity and intentness everywhere. At the time of prayer-services, rows of worshippers were formed both in the covered and uncovered parts of the mosque. Anyone who was a little late could not get a place in the congregation and if a person was not careful, he had to go the congregation and if a person was not careful he had to go without a sleeping space in the night.

Sheikhul Hadees Maulana Mohammad Zakaria had gone to Saharanpur for a few days to look after the Madrassa. When he returned, Maulana Abdul Qadir Raipuri, also, came with him which made the Maulana very happy, and he thanked Sheikhul Hadees profusely and blessed him for being the cause of Maulana Raipuri's visit.

Rumour

The people of Delhi were aware of the Seriousness of the Maulana's condition, and many of them visited him every day.

When those who had stayed for the night returned in the morning, their friends and relatives enquired from them anxiously about Maulana's welfare. One day, the rumour of his death spread like wildfire in the town, and people began arriving by every mode of transport. They came by cars, buses and Tongas in an unending stream. Innumerable telephone calls were received. The news was promptly contradicted, but it took time to have an effect. Thus, this Sunnat of the Apostle of God, also, was fulfilled. Maulana Mohammad Manzoor Nomani gave a forceful speech on the theme of "Mohammad is only an Apostle of God, and there have been many Apostles before him[1]." He said that, in reality, it was a warning to the citizens of Delhi. Those who had not yet paid heed and their worldly preoccupations had not given them the time to respond to the Maulana's call could still do so otherwise, though the news, at that time, was false, it would turn out to be true one day or the other.

Last days

A few showers had fallen two or three days before the Maulana's death, and there was a nip in the air. The Maulana's cot, at his insistence, used to be placed in the open for long hours as he felt a burning sensation all over the body. In consequence, he caught chill, which developed into Pneumonia. Unfortunately, it could not be detected in time.

On the 8th of July, at about 12 O'clock in the night, I had gone out for a stroll. On my return, I was told that the Maulana

---

[1] Adapted from Hazrat Abu Bakr's famous oration at the death of the holy prophet.

wanted to see me. I, at once, went to him and placed my ear close to his lips. For the first time, I felt that his voice was tremulous. He lapsed into unconsciousness frequently and had to utter every word twice or thrice before he could express himself. I do not remember exactly what he said, but it was an exhortation about Zikr and about sitting in the company of Maulana Raipuri.

At about 9 O'clock, on the next night, I happened to pass by the Maulana's apartment and saw that he was awake, and some attendants were doing something. I went in and sat down. After remaining unconscious for some time, the Maulana asked about someone whether he would go to his hometown and begin the Tabligh work. I replied that Insha Allah he would, and for the Maulana's satisfaction added that he was very influential there and his word would carry much weight. "Yes", the Maulana remarked. "Men of God possess the power to affect others," He, again, slipped into stupor, and on opening the eyes after some time, said, "It will be very good if a meeting can be held at Baghpat with the help of Molvi Tayyab (of Rampur Maniharaan), Molvi Zahirul Hasan (of Kandhla), and Hafiz Usman Khan (of Islamia College, Peshawar).

On the evening of Jul 10, the Maulana urged the Ulema to take part in the *Tabligh* movement that was worthy of their position.

On the morning of July 10, while drinking the water of Zam Zam, he recited the famous prayer of Hazrat Omar: "O God! Grant me martyrdom in Thy path and ordain death for me in the town of thy Prophet i.e., Medina."

On the same day, on seeing a gentleman, he said, "Ask him if he has conveyed the message of *Tabligh* to his community and what is he doing about it."

A physician who was in attendance told me that all the vital organs of the Maulana had stopped functioning, one by one, and it was only the strength of his heart that was keeping him alive. He, also, said that we should not judge about his condition by our own standards. What we were seeing was not physical but spiritual vitality.

On July 12, he sent the message to Sheikhul Hadees Maulana Mohammad Zakaria, Maulana Abdul Qadir Raipuri, and Maulana Zafar Ahmad that, among his men, he placed the greatest reliance upon Hafiz Maqbool Hasan, Qazi Dawood, Molvi Ihtishamul Hasan, Molvi Mohammad Yusuf, Molvi Inamul Hasan and Molvi Syed Raza Hasan, and they should have people who might be wanting to do the bait, perform it at the hand of anyone of them they considered most suitable. These gentlemen, thereupon, held consultations among themselves and informed the Maulana that they were in favour of Molvi Mohammad Yusuf as he fulfilled all the conditions laid down by Shah Waliullah in El-Qaul-ul-Jamil. He was well versed in Islamic sciences, and was a man of piety, and, also, kept steadily in touch with religious knowledge. The Maulana replied that if such was their choice, God would bless it. "I was greatly worried and had my misgivings," he added, "but now, I am satisfied. Insha Allah, the work will go on after me."

With the approach of the night, the Maulana had started getting ready for the last journey. He enquired if the next day was a Thursday and on being told that it was, he asked the attendants to see if there is trace of impurity on his clothes and was happy to learn that the clothes were clean. He, then, expressed the desire to get down from the cot and offer up Namaz with Wuzu, but was advised against it. The Maulana began the Isha Namaz with the congregation but had to abandon it owing to a sudden call of nature. He, then, said it with another congregation in his apartment. He wanted profusion in Dua[1] and Dam[2] in the night and said that only those stayed with him who could distinguish between the effects of the devil and the angels. He, then, asked Molvi Inamul Hasan how was the prayer, *Allahumma inna maghfiratika* and the latter helped him to recall it to his mind: *Allahumma inna maghfiratika ao sa'o min zunoobi wa rahmataka arja 'indi min 'amali.* (Oh God! Thy forgiveness is more extensive than mine inequities and I have better hope in Thy mercy than in my deeds). It remained on his lips constantly thereafter. He said he wished the attendants to give him a bath and take him down from the cot and let him offer two Rak'ats of Namaz, and then see what fruits it bore.

Denoting the act of reciting the Name of Allah or a prayer for the recovery of one who is sick. and then. driving air upon him.

At about 12 O'clock in the night, the Maulana had an attack of restlessness. The doctor was summoned, who administered some medicines. Sounds of Allah-o-Akbar, Allah-o-Akbar were heard rising from his throat. Towards the morning, he sent for Molvi Mohammad Yusuf and Molvi Ikramul Hasan and when they came, he said to the former, "Come. Let me embrace you. I am going. "The end came a little before the morning Azan.

---

[1] Meaning prayer and supplication.

The tired and weary traveller had, at last, arrived at the journey's end.

The succession ceremony of Maulana Mohammad Yusuf was performed in the morning, and in the midst of tears, the Maulana's tiara was tied to his head.

Bathing of the dead body, shrouding, and burial

The bathing of the dead body began soon after. It was done with their own hands. by the theologians and legists. When perfume was being applied to the limbs of prostration, Haji Abdur Rahman remarked that it should be done liberally on the forehead which remained placed on the ground, in *Sajda,* for long stretches of time.

Within minutes, the news of the Maulana's death had reached Delhi, and people had started pouring in from all sides. A large crowd had gathered. Maulana Mohammad Zakaria and Maulana Mohammad Yusuf said that people should be told to collect in the open space below and someone should speak to them. What better theme could there be for the occasion than that "Mohammad is only an Apostle of God, and there have been many Apostles before him."

Maulana Zafar Ahmad and Mufti Kifayatullah spoke in the same vein and counselled fortitude and steadfastness.

By the Zuhr service. The crowed had exceeded all limits. There were so many people performing Wuzu that the water level of the tank fell. Not an inch of vacant space was to be found in the mosque, both on the ground and upper floors. When the bier was brought out for the funeral Namaz, the crowd became unmanageable. Poles had to be attached to it to enable the people to lend a shoulder. With much difficulty, the bier was taken to the grave. Sheikhul Hadees led the service, and the bier was taken back to the mosque for burial. It was extremely difficult to make one's way into the mosque. People scaled the walls with the help of ropes. The grave had been dug in the eastern corner of the mosque, by the side of the graves of the Maulana's father and brother. The dead body was, finally, lowered in the grave. By the end of the day, the 'sun' that had illumined the hearts of millions of men and spread the warmth of Faith in all directions had disappeared in the earth.

Survivors

The Maulana left behind only one daughter who was married to his nephew and favourite pupil, Sheikhul Hadees Maulana Mohammad Zakaria.

Pen portrait

The Maulana's complexion was wheatish. He was short-statured, and his body was frail, but he was full of energy and had an enormous capacity for work. He was never idle. His beard was thick and dark with a few grey hairs which could be seen only when one looked closely. He had a thoughtful look, and his face bore the marks of life- long abstinence, moral and spiritual discipline and worshipfulness, and the forehead indicated high-mindedness and magnanimity. He used to stammer a little, but his voice was powerful, and manner of speaking, forceful and impassioned.

Chapter VII:
Distinctive qualities

Among the main, distinctive qualities of Maulana Mohammad Ilyas were Iman and *Ihtisab*. What these terms denote, briefly, is that one performed an act with fullest faith in God as the Supreme Being, the Knower and Creator of all things, and in confident expectation of the reward and recompense promised on it.

It is stated in the Traditions:

> "Whoever will keep the fasts of Ramzan with Iman and *Ihtisab*, all his previous sins will be forgiven." (Bukhari)
>
> "Whoever will keep vigil during Shab-i-Qadr (The Night of Power) with Iman and *Ihtisab*, all his previous sins will be forgiven." (Bukhari).
>
> It is related by Abdullah bin Amr bin el-Aas that the Apostle of God said: "There are forty things, the foremost among which is that a person gave his goat to someone to help himself with its milk and to return it (when it became day). Whoever will do any of these things in the hope of earning the Divine reward and with faith in and affirmation of the promise of the Lord on it, the Lord will let him enter Paradise." (Bukhari)

The Maulana attached the greatest importance to these attributes of Faith and did his best to revive the spirit of Iman and *Ihtisab* in the Millet. Extracts reproduced below from his letters will show how particular he was about it.

(i) "The essence of Faith lies in Iman and *Ihtisab*. These are distinctly mentioned in respect of many acts. To ponder over the commandments relating to them, and, through it, to strengthen the awareness of the glory of the Lord and belief in the earthly and heavenly rewards and benefits promised on those deeds-that is the thing."

(ii) "Deeds, by themselves, do not possess any value. Value is produced as a result of attachment to God through compliance with His commands. The real worth and value of the deeds will, as such, depends on the extent of control over the cause of this attachment and it will be proportionate to the willingness of the heart and strength of the conviction with which these are performed."

(iii) "I feel envious at the absence of fervour and enthusiasm you have mentioned. For the Believer the reality of compliance with the command of God is that he should be so overwhelmed with faith in the command that it subdued his enthusiasm. Enthusiasm is from heart. If there is enthusiasm, it will stem from the love of the hearts, and if it stems from willing obedience to the Command of the Lord, it will be mental and religious love."

(iv) "Sometimes, joy at doing a little becomes a barrier to the realisation of the inability to do the rest, and you must be on guard against the deception. From the joy of the doers, we should learn to abstain from the folly of regarding the effects produced by our efforts to be a measure of our success. The real fruit of a religious act is reward and recompense, and it is related only to remaining engaged in work. What, then, can it have to do with worldly effects? Anyhow, if the effects are taking place, we should simply believe that the effects we are, fallaciously, looking for in this world, also, are materialising. We should strive even if no effects are felt. To slacken the efforts when the effects begin to appear are felt. To slacken the efforts when the effects begin to appear is a great mistake. Our endeavour should, therefore, be to realise our faults and negligence."

(v) "We should observe all the duties of worship and remembrance of God with a full regard for the rules and proprieties and a complete reliance upon the promises made on them. It is a great thing to persuade ourselves to believe in those promises. Since it is related to the heart, it occupies the place of the heart in the design of worship, and spirituality is related to it."

(vi) "To know the merit and superiority of the time prescribed for each of the acts of worship and to believe in it and observe those acts at the proper time is the way in which they should be performed. The virtues of the stipulated hours have been described in the Traditions, and these hours have their own radiance. For commoners like us, it is enough that while offering up Namaz at the prescribed time, we prayed to God to grant us a share in the propitiousness of that particular time."

(vii) "Do not bother about joy or satisfaction but go on observing the duties with a full awareness of the commands of God and attaching the greatest importance to their fulfilment. The observance of the command and willing obedience to the order is a very great thing."

The entire endeavour of the Maulana revolved around Iman and *Ihtisab*, i.e., the propitiation of the Lord, through it, and making oneself worthy of the boundless reward promised on obeying the Prophet, and guiding men towards goodness, and making a provision for the Hereafter. In a letter, he says:

The method of *Tabligh* is partly related to the heart, and, partly, to the external organs. Some of the things that are related to the heart are:

(i) The feeling that the object of going from place to place in this work is to follow the example of the leader of the Apostles, the Prophet Mohammad, and to propitiate the Lord by means of it.

(ii) The awareness of the dictum that whoever guides a person to virtue is like him who practices it, and the belief that in whatever degree people devoted themselves, through one's efforts, to Namaz, Zikr and recitation of the Quran, the good deeds done by each one of them were one's own provision for the Hereafter and the keeping in mind, in detail, of the reward promised on all those acts.

(iii) Cultivation of the strength of prayer and supplication, and beseeching of the Lord, at each step, with unswerving faith in His Omniscience and Benevolence, for success in *Tabligh* and for His countenance.

(iv) Gratitude to the Lord believing that one's participation in the noble task was solely due to His favour.

(v) Behaving habitually towards the Muslims with humility and politeness."

In another letter, he writes:

"The act or means of serving the cause of Faith become lasting when a person keeps the happenings of the Last Day before his mind's eye and believes that the rewards, as promised by the holy Prophet, on those deeds will be his provision in the life to come (provided that they found acceptance with the Lord).

"The more this conviction will grow, the more will the Almighty bestow the sweetness of Faith on the bondsman, and the more the sweetness of Faith is gained, the keener will be the eagerness. For instance, find out what is the reward in the Shariat on the defaulters who have become regular in Namaz through your efforts, and be sure, that all this is going to be yours in the Hereafter.

"Meditate upon the Day of Resurrection, with faith in the reality of it and in the truth that such a Day shall befall you. Further, affirm the Apostleship of the sacred Prophet from the bottom of your heart, and remember that only what he has told is going to serve you in the Afterlife." On another occasion, he wrote:

"Striving for the glory of the Word of God and the propagation of the Revelation should solely be done in the spirit of compliance with His will and for winning His good pleasure and with the belief that it was going to be a provision for the hereafter. The favour promised by the Lord is related to such a life alone, as is borne out by thousands of verses of the Quran like, Lo! Those who believe, and those who emigrate (for the sake of God) and strive in the way of Allah, these have hope of Allah's mercy. Allah is Forgiving, Merciful. (II:218).

"Believing in the self to be so dirty, ugly and ruinous that, aside of the mercy of the lord, it cannot be corrected and reformed till death, you should try and propagate the teachings of the Prophet with the intention that, in addition to you, whatever religious work will be done by pious and virtuous bondmen will be a good work, both outwardly and inwardly, and the Lord may, by His Infinite Benevolence, grant you, also, a share in it in conformity' with the maxim that *whoever guides a person to virtue is like him who practices it*."

Laying stress on meditation, the Maulana says:

"There is nothing very difficult about reflection. and meditation. What it denotes, simply, is that one sat in solitude and told one's inner self that this thing was, definitely, pleasing to God, and death which was bound to come at the appointed time would, certainly, set right one's carnal life, and putting one's trust in the dictum that *whoever guides a person to virtue is like him who practices it*, added together all the virtues that accrued or could accrue from going out for *Tabligh*, and associated the countenance of the Lord with them with effort and with an unqualified faith this is reflection."

The Maulana wanted the relatives of the people who went out and travelled from place to place for *Tabligh*, also, to associate themselves with their work and join in the recompense by encouraging them and bearing the separation with good cheer. He wished to produce the attitudes of Iman and *Ihtisab* and eagerness for reward and recompense in the whole of the Millet. Making a beginning with his own family, he wrote to his relatives from Arabia:

"Imagine for what a long time people leave their homes for worldly aims and interests. At this very moment, thousands of Muslims who are serving in the armies of the Infidels are ready to lay down their lives and depart from the world forever merely for the sake of the stomach. You must not be so faint-hearted. If you bear the separation, resulting from my exertions in the path of Faith cheerfully and resolutely, you will have a share in the reward in proportion to the willingness. You should consider yourselves lucky that your relatives are undergoing hardship in the service of Faith and be grateful to the Lord for it. The reward on this hardship will be endless. You will be requited bounteously for every loss or injury suffered in the course of it."

In the Maulana's view there was no better and surer source of reward for a weak and busy person, with all his limitations, in this brief existence than to engage himself in *Tabligh* and guide the others to virtue with Iman and *Ihtisab*. Even a person who fasts during the day and spends the nights in prayer and completes the recital of the Quran every day or gives away lakhs of rupees in charity cannot equal in effulgence and profusion the reward that is reaching those, uninterruptedly, through the obligatory prayers, faith and religious conduct of countless of men who attained guidance and were led to good-doing by their efforts. The conduct, strength, and earnestness of any individual cannot compare with the conduct, strength, and earnestness of hundreds of men. That is why the Maulana considered. The endeavour for collective moral and religious uplift to be more precious than individual devoutness. The Maulana counselled a holy person who had grown old and had performed great deeds in his life, through a friends, that now that he did not possess enough strength to exert himself and the time was short and there was so much to be done, prudence demanded that he became the means of the good-doing of others and drew the attention of his friends towards *Tabligh* through conversation and correspondence.

Apart from regarding the *Tabligh* movement the easiest and most reliable source of Iman and *Ihtisab*, the Maulana's preoccupation with the idea was so complete that he hardly took a step without the intention of Divine reward or hope of religious gain. His every thought, act and movement was governed by it. It was with this aim and object that he talked, took part in a function or ceremony, showed anger or expressed joy. In the words of Maulana Mohammad Manzoor Nomani, "He, perhaps, never took or offered a cup of tea without having the Divine recompense in view."

The Maulana took care to formulate the intention of deriving the utmost religious gain from every act or occasion and turning it into a means of seeking the countenance of God. He would elevate worldly deeds into acts of worship. He had a knack, bordering on the genius, for guiding people towards the special reward or advantage, according to their levels, through different aims and intentions for the same act. It is related by Maulana Mohammad Manzoor Nomani that "I reached Nizamuddin once in the afternoon, during the last days of the Maulana's mortal illness. He could hardly sit up in bed. Some Mewati attendants were helping him to perform Wuzu for the Zuhr prayer-service. As he saw me, he motioned me to himself and said:

> "Molvi: Saheb! Though Hazrat Abdullah bin Abbas had seen the holy Prophet performing Wuzu for years, and so, also, had he seen Hazrat Abu Bakr and Hazrat Omar, for his own education, he used to observe Hazrat Ali's Wuzu.'
>
> "When, after it, I saw the Maulana performing Wuzu, I felt that we could learn a great deal from his Wuzu about how it

was to be done during illness. The Maulana, then, pointed out towards the Mewati attendants and said:

"They are helping me to perform Wuzu, and I say to them that they love me and care for me for the sake of God, and think that I offer a better Namaz than them. So, they should help me to perform Wuzu with the intention of having a share in the reward on my Namaz. On my part. I make this prayer: O Allah! These simple-minded bondmen of Thine have such a high opinion of me, let them not be disappointed. Accept my Namaz, and grant them, also a share in it."

The Maulana added:

"If I feel that my Namaz is superior to their Namaz in the sight of God, He will reject me, and I will fall from His grace. My only hope is that because of these plain and trustful bondmen, God will not refuse to accept my Namaz."

Now look what ways of earning the wealth of Faith through intention did the Maulana open for the three parties of different states concerned in a single action. For Maulana Nomani, the virtue of knowledge and adherence to the confirmed practice of the sacred Prophet, and through it, the reward on the intention of perfecting his Wuzu; for the Mewatis, a share in the reward on Namaz of the grade of Ihsan; and for himself, the acceptance of Namaz as a result of the good opinion of the Mewatis. Without Iman and Ihtisab, it would have been nothing more than an ordinary Wuzu.

The State of Ihsan

In the Traditions, Ihsan has been described as "to worship God as if you saw Him, for if you do not see Him, be sure, He sees you." Maulana Mohammad Ilyas was an embodiment of this state. Even in company, his condition was as if he was in the presence of the Lord. Maulana Mohammad Manzoor Nomani has correctly said, and my own observation confirms it, that "he often recited the following prayer so feelingly that it appeared that he was actually uttering it before the Throne of the Almighty: *O God, with Thy glorification and Thy praise. I attest that there is no God save Thee. Thou art one and without a partner. I beg Thy forgiveness, and to Thee do I turn penitent. O Thou, Living, Eternal One, unto Thy Mercy do 1 appeal. Set right my condition and leave me not to the self even for a moment.*

Image of the Last Day and the Hereafter

In the same way, the image of the Last Day and the Hereafter was so vividly drawn before his mind's eye that it reminded one of Hazrat Rabia Basri's remark about the Companions that their awareness of the Day of Resurrection was so real and intense as if they had seen it with their own eyes. Once, the Maulana asked a Mewati what had brought him to Delhi. The Mewati replied that he had come to see the town, and then, realising from the Maulana's reaction that he had made a mistake, said that he had come to offer up Namaz in Jam'i Masjid, and, then, again, he changed his statement and said that he had come to pay his respects to him. Upon it, the Maulana observed, 'What are Delhi and Jam'i Masjid as compared to paradise and what am I that you should come to see me? I am at mere structure of flesh and bones that is destined to perish one day." Then, as the Maulana proceeded to describe Heaven, it appeared that it was present right there before him.

Faith in the transitoriness of the world and the reality and permanence of the Hereafter had become a part of his being so much so that it found expression even in his friendly conversation and letters. Once, the Maulana said to me that "we would be meeting in Lucknow", and then, hurriedly added, "What meeting can there be in a journey? We will, Insha Allah, be meeting in the Hereafter."

Once while consoling Maulana Mohammad Talha on the death of his wife, the Maulana said, "The reality of the world is only this much that you first shut one leaf of a door, and then, the other. People depart from here in the same way, one after the other."

Absorption

The Maulana's absorption is his work was so complete that he had little time or inclination for anything else in the world.

As he once wrote to Sheikhul Hadees Maulana Mohammad Zakaria: "My earnest desire is that my mind, heart, strength and time were devoted to no other thing than this work."

Sometimes, he would say, "How is it proper for me to spend my time and energy on any other thing when I see that the soul of the sacred Prophet is unhappy (owing to the moral and religious degeneration of Muslims)"

One day, an attendant complained that the Maulana did not have the same affection for him as he had earlier.

The Maulana replied, "I am very busy. I feel that the Prophet is unhappy, so how can I pay attention to anything else?"

He would compare himself to the policeman who stood at a crossing, regulating the traffic. Other things, too, were important, but he could not leave his place. It would be disastrous.

Once while passing through New Delhi, Maulana Mohammad Nazim of Nadwa enquired from him about an important building, "I have no knowledge of these things," the Maulana replied:

He avoided going to functions at which he felt he would not get an opportunity to serve the cause. He used to advise his friends and colleagues to take with them the message of *Tabligh* wherever they went and give the highest priority to it.

It was tiring for the Maulana if he had to listen to an aimless talk. Occasionally, he would tell the speaker, bluntly, to stop, and if he had to bear it, against his will, one could easily feel his discomfort. Once during a journey, one of the companions began to talk to another in a general way. As the conversation progressed, the Maulana told them quietly to go and sit at some other place.

Even when the Maulana went to Kandhla, his hometown, or was with his relatives, he did not miss an opportunity to put forward his viewpoint. But he did it in such a subtle way that the listeners did not feel bored or irritated. Once the Maulana had to attend a marriage party at a friend's place in Delhi when, in the midst of rejoicing, he said, "Today is a day of great joy for you on, which even the menials are made happy and the sweepress, too, is not overlooked. Now, tell me what you have done for the satisfaction of the sacred Prophet?" He, then, dwelt on *Tabligh* as the surest means to please the Prophet and called upon everyone to join in the endeavour he had launched.

The Maulana seldom wrote a letter for any other purpose, and when he had to do so, he, invariably, began with a reference to his mission, and then, moved on to the matter in hand. A Mewati student requested him, in my presence, to write a recommendatory letter to Maulana Tayyab Saheb of Deoband. The letter dictated by the Maulana was mostly about *Tabligh* and only the last two or three lines contained the recommendation.

When I went to visit my relatives, the Maulana always enquired on my return if I had spoken to them about the *Tabligh* movement and asked them to join it. If my reply happened to be in the negative, he would say: "Maulana! Unless ties and relationships come under the feet of the Prophet, they are dead."

In a letter of invitation about a marriage in his own family, the Maulana wrote: "In these days of widespread degeneration, I regard gatherings on such occasions to be a sign of the apathy and indifference of the Muslims, but as our elders, Ulema and spiritual mentors are going to attend it, I request all of my friends to come and have a share in the blessings of both the worlds and give this humble bondsman an opportunity to explain the *Tabligh* programme."

In his view, everything in which there was no gain of Faith was a waste of time. Once I was listening with interest to an incident that had taken place in a *Tabligh* journey. As the Maulana heard it, he remarked, "It is past history. Talk about something useful."

The Maulana placed a great value on time, and it made him sad to see it wasted. Once the mail was being attended to when an old letter that had got mixed up came to hand, and it took a few minutes to discover that it had already been seen. The Maulana said: "Tear it, otherwise it will, again, take up our time unnecessarily. Time Is our commodity."

Love of purpose

The Maulana had, once, described love as concentration, on any one object of the Joys and interests that were distributed among so many things around us. This definition applied perfectly to his own case in respect of Faith. He had fallen in love with Faith, with his heart and soul, and before it, all other attachment and inclinations had faded into insignificance. He derived the same freshness and strength from it as one does from food and water. When a *Tabligh* worker complained to him of uneasiness, he said, "the *Tabligh* work, in fact, is the spiritual food of man. By His grace, God had favoured you with it. Now, it is natural to feel uneasy at its temporary diminution." Do not worry."

Many a time did it happen that the Maulana forgot his illness on receiving good news regarding the *Tabligh* movement or on meeting someone he considered useful for it. In the same way, he suffered a distinct setback if a discouraging thing took place. All his worries had got lost in that one worry as he, himself, once, wrote: "Apart from the pain of *Tabligh*, all is well with me.

Sometimes, he would say: "I have no desire for food owing to pre-occupation (with *Tabligh*). I simply sit down at the meal with others or eat when the time comes."

The Maulana waited eagerly for the arrival. of *Tabligh* parties. To a worker who was bringing a *Jama'at* he, once, wrote: "I am waiting for the *Jama'at* which will come along the bank of Jamuna with the same keenness with which people try to see the I'd moon. Bring the Jama'at with utmost care."

During his last illness, the Maulana had grown so weak that, sometimes, even a thing of joy proved too much for him. In January 1944, as a Jama'at came from Lucknow, the Maulana said to me after the Fajr service that the work at Kanpur would, probably, have stopped on his return. He had, perhaps, received reports to that effect. I told him that a Jama'at had gone to Kanpur from Lucknow and the work had started again. Pointing towards Haji Wali Mohammad, I said that he, too, was in the party. The Maulana stretched his hands towards him for a handshake and kissed his hand. He said, "My head has begun to ache with joy. Do not make me overjoyed. I have no strength left even for it."

Likewise, he, sometimes, fell ill owing to a lapse on the part of the Jama'at. Once he told me that he had been taken ill on returning from Saharanpur, and when I enquired about the reason, he explained, "The Jama'at that came from other places did not observe the rules. They wasted their time on sightseeing."

The following extracts from a letter of his may be worth reproducing:

"We have to produce men who can sacrifice their worldly possessions and even life for the sake of *Tabligh* and make *Tabligh* the sole object of their existence. It is necessary to lay down one's life willingly in this path.

"Had they, with faith in the dictum the God does not allow the reward of those who do good to be wasted and the aspiration to be called fanatics in this path, believed that death in these endeavours was life itself, they would have tasted the pleasures of Heaven even in this existence."

The Maulana, indeed, felt the joy of Paradise in the hardship he had to endure for *Tabligh*. The hot winds of summer appeared more pleasant to him than the gentle breeze of the morning. Once, in the last week of May, he was going by car to Qutub Saheb with Maulana

Mohammad Zakaria, Molvi Ikramul Hasan and the present writer. The Maulana asked the windows of the car to be shut as strong gusts of hot wind were coming in upon which Sheikhul Hadees, humorously, remarked, "Yes, now the hot wind is hurting. Had it been a *Tabligh* journey, it would have mattered nothing." "Of course,", replied the Maulana.

Whenever he saw an exceptionally intelligent or capable man, his first thought was how his talents could be utilised for *Tabligh.* In a letter to Maulana Mohammad Zakaria, from Arabia, he wrote I received Hakim Rasheed's Letter and was struck by his intellectual faculties. I was tempted to feel how gifted men God had given to our family. If only these people use their talents for what they are really meant, they can surpass even those who are in the front-line in the service of Faith. The same way did I feel on reading the poem of Mian Faraghat."

Dr. Zakir Husain tells that, once, during the Maulana's illness, some filth got stuck to his back. In washing it away, there was the risk of his getting wet and catching cold. No one knew how the Maulana could be cleansed without giving him a bath. Maulana Yusuf, then, poured water over it from the spout of a lota in such a way that the filth was removed without wetting the body The Maulana was greatly pleased. He blessed Maulana Mohammad Yusuf and said, "this skill and intelligence should be employed in the service of Faith."

Anxiety

No one who did not see the Maulana could imagine the extent of his agony. Sometimes, he would groan: "Oh God! What am I to do? I am good for nothing." He got up in the night and paced up and down the room. On one such night, his wife asked, "What is the matter? Why don't you sleep?" "If you knew, two would be awake instead of one."

In a letter he wrote: "I find no comparison between my anxiety, my effort, and my voice, and the responsibility of *Tabligh* God has placed on my shoulders. If He shows mercy, He is Forgiving, Merciful, and if He does justice, there is no escape for me from the consequences of my guilt."

The feeling of dejection became intense when the Maulana saw that the forces of godlessness were closing in from all sides, and his Movement was not making much headway. As he wrote to a friend:

"Your letter reached me a few days ago. It should have done good to my heart, but my friend, the tide of mischief and irreligiousness is running faster than an express train while the *Tabligh* movement which, alone, can turn darkness into light, is advancing very slowly, at the pace of an ant." On another line A another letter of his reads:

"You have written about *Tabligh* activities. You say that eighty persons came to your place for *Tabligh,* and a *Jama'at* of twenty-five workers was ready to leave. The first news is most pleasing. It is a great favour of the Lord that as many as eighty men left their homes for the preaching and propagation of the Faith at a time when nobody cares for it. But my friends, along with the expression of gratitude to the Lord, we should, also, feel ashamed that after 15 years of striving and observing the blessedness of *Tabligh* with our own eyes, only 80 persons, out of millions of Muslims, could set out of their homes, and they, too, were so eager to return that it took a lot of effort to hold them back. When it is so hard to persuade them to go out on a *Tabligh* tour, and even after it, the perishable home pulls them back, how will the Faith flourish? As long as stay at home does not become as difficult as it is now to set out in the path of *Tabligh* and to return home is not as painful as it is now to leave it, and you do not make the travel from place to place, for the sake of *Tabligh*, a part of the life of your community, the community will not experience the real flavour of Faith nor enjoy the fruits of true religiousness."

In yet another letter, he wrote:

"What I mean is that until the male members of every family made it a duty to stay away from home, turn by turn, for serving the cause of Faith", e., *Tabligh*, devotion to Faith must remain a dream.

"Just imagine, the whole family is engaged in worldly pursuits and the call is given for only one of its members to set out in the path of Faith-and even this is not done! Is it not placing a lesser value on the Hereafter than on this world? Look at those Jama'ats. Have all of them not returned home within a few days of your sending the news of their departure? My joy over the setting out of Jama'ats does not die down that reports start coming that they have returned."

Struggle

I was quite common to serve the cause of Faith through the pen and the tongue, but to put forth great physical efforts for it was the unique contribution of the Maulana in the present time. He prayed himself for steadfastness in the path he had chosen as well as begged the chosen bondmen of the Lord to do the same. For instance, the Maulana wrote to Sheikhul Hadees Maulana Mohammad Zakaria:

"I beg you most sincerely to pray that this. endeavour of mine remains oriented to action from beginning to end, and that the profusion of words is not allowed to impair its spirit, and speech is intended only to help it forward."

The Maulana used to say, "the basic purpose of my Movement is to revive the tradition of laying down one's life in the path of Islam." In spite of persistent ill-health, he spared no pains to carry out the task he had undertaken. Sometimes, he covered as many as 25 miles in a day, on foot, during the tours of Mewat. He would not find time to eat for 36 or even 48 hours, although the food was with him. On several occasions, he left Nizamuddin on a Thursday night or Friday morning, after having his meal, and ate again only on returning to it on Sunday. He kept awake in the nights, crossed hilly ranges, traversed difficult paths, and bore with equal equanimity the hot winds of May and June and the chilly air of December and January in the open wasteland of Mewat. He used to encourage the companions by saying. "On the other side of toil and hardship is God. Whoever wants may come and meet Him."

He undertook the tours of Mewat in intense heat and a very poor state of health, but it mattered little to him for he considered those journeys to be the journeys of Jehad and the desert of Mewat, the battlefield. About one of these tours, he wrote, in May 1930, to Maulana Mohammad Zakaria, and his own son, Maulana Mohammad Yusuf:

"I feel so exhausted that a confused talk or anything that is opposed to my nature irritates me, and even a comfortable journey by car gives me fever. In spite of all this, I am determined, by the grace of God, to make a month-long tour of Mewat in this biting cold and subjecting myself to the rambling and disjointed conversation of Illiterate people. But, considering the journey to be a journey of Jehad, I have made up my mind to invite death by undertaking it.

From my utter prostration and low-spiritedness, I, however, fear that I may quail before the ordeal and decide to abandon the journey and return in humiliation. So, pray that God may grant me the courage to bear those hardships, even to the extent of dying, or bring me back safely on completing the task. I am setting out on the tour as an important duty, without any hope of returning alive, yet I believe that it would be the worst type of sin if I showed concern for my well-being."

Once, the Maulana was travelling up a mountainous road in a bullock cart when the cart overturned at Kultajpur, and the passengers were injured. They managed to reach the top with much difficulty. There was some Ulema, also, in the party who were not accustomed to hardship, but before anyone could complain, the Maulana changed their mood with the remark, "Friends, today, for the first time in your life, you have faced an ascent like that of Hira. Now, tell me, how many times did the Prophet do that?" After it, who had the heart to grumble?

Nothing could deter him once he had made up his mind. He never gave way to despair. Once he thought of something which had to be told to the people of Nooh, and left Nizamuddin on foot at 4 O'clock in the morning. At Delhi, he borrowed Haji Nasim's car and reached Nooh when the town was still asleep. Occasionally, during a tour a Mewat it rained heavily, and the roads were flooded. The Maulana decided to go to some place at that very time and reached his destination in knee-deep water. Brushing aside all opposition and refusing the offer of the hosts to arrange for a Tonga.

Maulana Mohammad Manzoor Nomani has aptly remarked that "though the Maulana was extremely frail of body, he put up such a tremendous effort for *Tabligh* that I think if Paradise with all its boons and comforts and Hell with all its penalties and torments were revealed to anyone and it was said to him that if he did such-and-such a thing, he would get Paradise, otherwise he would be cast into Hell, he would, perhaps, not strive harder for it than what Maulana Mohammad Ilyas had done, particularly during the last phase of his life."

At the same time, he was highly solicitous of the comfort of follow workers and never put them to unnecessary hardship. He thought of ways to make things easier for them along with preparing them ceaselessly for the struggle.

Once, during a tour of Mewat, he told his colleagues to labour hard, and with it, asked the Mewatis to look after their comfort. He, then, said to the workers, "If only comfort falls to your lot, you will be the losers."

On his own part, the Maulana did not spurn the facilities God provided for him not treated them as of no value, but regarded them to be the gifts of the Lord and a blessing. He neither craved for them nor refused to accept what came to him without asking.

The Maulana was not one of those who derive a morbid pleasure from suffering and prefer the harder to the easier course merely for the sake of it. In the path of Faith, he exhorted the people to keep their spirits high in the midst of all sorts of difficulties and tribulations. To the Mewati *Moballighs* going out on a *Tabligh* mission his advice was not to abandon the rugged simplicity that was a most valuable attribute of their way of living. They should eat plain food, sleep on the floor and cultivate the habits of toil and hardiness.

He used to say that man had been made for work. If he did not exert in the path of Faith, he would turn towards worldly interests, as the case was in those days. While man was moving the earth and the sky for petty and doubtful gains of the world, would it be too much to bear some hardship for a positive thing like the reward of the Hereafter. Once, on receiving the news of a colleague's illness, he said, "It is not much if one develops fever as a result of striving in the path of Faith when lives are being laid down for bread."

High mindedness

Another notable characteristic of the Maulana was magnanimity and high-mindedness. The task to which he had dedicated his life did not blend with the environment. It was much above the general moral and intellectual level of the times. He, therefore, was very careful in placing his aims and ideals before the people. Once, he sorrowfully said to Molvi Zahirul Hasan, "No one understands what is in my heart. They think that this movement is Salat[1], But I swear it is not so," On another occasion, he said to him, "Zahirul Hasan, we aim to create a new Ummat."[2]

He did not consider his endeavour to be a passing phase. It was not even acceptable to him that its effects lasted for a few centuries, and no more. He wanted it to be a permanent movement of religious instruction and reform. As he wrote to me:

"Your ambitious letter gave me much joy. May God make the information conform to facts and impart such solidity and permanence to the Movement that it lasts forever and does not turn out to be a momentary ebullition and dies out after a few centuries. Please pray for the strength and stability of its foundations."

---

[1] Meaning regular worship.

[2] Meaning a community.

Maulana Nasrullah relates that once he said to Maulana Mohammad Ilyas that some people regarded him to be the Mujaddid (Renovator) of the day. "Who told you?" The Maulana asked. "People are saying it," replied Maulana Nasrullah. "No" he observed, "My *Jama'ats* is the Mujaddid."

Similarly, the Maulana, once, said that he prayed to God that the *Tabligh* movement did not thrive on the supernatural otherwise men would be tempted to associate it with a particular person or era while what he wanted was that people, at all times and in all ages, came forward to serve it and kept it going. He wanted *Tabligh* to become a permanent way of life with the Muslims. It was not enough to bring about a change in the morals and habits of the Mewatis. He wished them, also, to change their language and adopt Arabic. Nothing was impossible, in his view, with the help of God and human endeavour. He even hoped for the revival of the Arabic language in the Madrassas. As he once wrote to me, "There are some ideas in my mind, which I do not want to express because they are too advanced. I would like you to consider seriously the possibility of the students talking to each other in Arabic in these days of *Tabligh*."

He was not willing to see the Movement confined to India. In his mind he had prepared a plan to carry the message of *Tabligh* to the whole world, specially the Arab and Islamic countries, and, sometimes, spoke about it with rare feeling He had very, high hopes from that the work he had launched. The infeasible and the. impracticable meant little to him. He strove to the utmost and entreated the Lord with all his heart and considered nothing to be beyond His Power. In a letter to Sheikhul Hadees Maulana Mohammad Zakaria, he wrote:

"I request you most humbly, and in the name of God and the Apostle, to give up your notions of impossibility with regard to this work and consider it to be easy of accomplishment. My friends, to look at the world instead of the Might of the Lord in matters that are between God and the world and between the Creator and the creatures and give thought to depressing causes instead of the rousing Words of the Almighty is not worthy of men of vision. The eternal laws of God are proclaiming at trumpet's tune that you will get what you beg for and expect confidently from Him. Then, why should men of understanding like you not keep on entreating Him with eyes fixed on the feelings of the Prophet Mohammad?"

Religious pride

Religious pride was ingrained in Maulana's nature. One of the main reasons of his anxiety and over-powering urge to make the *Tabligh* movement a powerful instrument of religious revival was the ever-increasing ascendency of apostasy and godlessness, which a self-respecting person like him could not tolerate ever for a moment. But he did not like to make any change in the plan of *Tabligh* he had in mind under a momentary impulse. He, therefore, bore such things with equanimity, but, sometimes, gave vent to feeling, which showed what a storm was raging in his heart.

Once while passing by the Red Fort, I enquired from the Maulana if he had ever visited it. The Maulana replied, "I regard it shameful to visit the Red Fort. I had gone into it once in childhood when the guides to take us round with tears in their eyes."

Of the places, which bore witness to the past glory of the Muslims, he used to say that it was dangerous for one's faith to pass by them without reciting Qurioot-i-Naazila.

I pained him to see the examinations of Oriental studies being conducted by the Universities. He used to say that owing to it, one's mental outlook underwent a change, and in the place of God, the relation of religious knowledge was established with the world. He did not want the Muslims to be dependent upon others for the acquisition of religious knowledge or learning the Arabic language. In a letter to Molvi Abdul Latif, he said, "I feel ashamed that infidels should be the examiners of the Muslims in Arabic."

Repudiation of a commandant of the Shariat or its rejection as unjust or obsolete was extremely repugnant to him. Writing about Mewat to Maulana Abdul Latif of Saharanpur, in a similar situation, he said:

"It must be impressed upon the Mewatis that it was essential to subordinate their Panchayats and their trade to the dictates of the Shariat and that they took all the decisions in that light and considered it to be the essence of Islam otherwise their faith was most defective, and, sometimes, it was destroyed altogether and became pure Infidelity owing to the disregard or repudiation of the laws of the Shariat.

"Included among these is the *Istinkaf*[1] of Nikah (marriage) by choice, which, I hear, was earlier regarded by them as forbidden and un-Islamic, but now, though they say that it is legitimate, in the hearts, the position is the same. Thus, in the village of Atawar of Tehsil Nooh, a couple had its Nikah performed by mutual choice at some other place fearing that if it did so in its own village or tehsil, its community would punish it. Thereafter, the couple took up residence in Gurgaon, but its community did not forgive it, and they

---

[1] Meaning to feel ashamed of; to loathe; to detest.

killed the husband (whose Nikah was performed on the last Friday of the month of Ramzan) on the third day of I'd which, also, happened to be a Friday, cut the dead body into pieces and burnt it the down and threw the ashes into river. It is necessary to speak forcefully on the subject that Infidelity, Polytheism and adultery and fornication and other grievous sins are not held so wicked and detestable while a thing that has been sanctioned by God is regarded hateful to such an extent. You must emphasise how Faith can survive in these circumstances and is there any way of protecting it when they act like that?"

A measure of his pride of Faith was that he stoutly fought against the Shuddhi Sanghatan movement that was launched, in the twenties, by the Arya Samajists for the conversion of Muslims to Hinduism and did not allow it to make any headway in Mewat.

Observance of the Sunnat

The Maulana had few equals so far as keenness to abide by the Sunnat[1] was concerned. His eagerness to follow the example of the Prophet in all the spheres of li e revived the memory of the pious precursors. To search for and act upon even the minor Sunnats, to draw the attention of the others to them, and to regard the less important saying and practices of the holy Prophet, also, to be of great value came natural to him. Even on the last day of his life he said to Maulana Mohammad Zakaria, "I exhort you to do your best to learn about the actions. Habits and morals of the sacred Prophet from the Traditions and to follow and propagate them." To the

[1] Literally Sunnat means 'precedent' or 'custom', but it has been used exclusively by the Maulana to denote the sayings and doings of the Prophet Mohammad.

attendants who were not present at that time, he sent a message through Haji Abdur Rahman in which the foremost stress was laid on adherence to Sunnat.

The personal habits of the Maulana, too, bore the imprint of his anxiety to emulate the example of the Prophet. He wished to follow him even in matters of natural inclination. As he came to the mosque during his last illness, supported by two men, he ardently desired that in it, too, there was the same spirit that had been related in the Traditions concerning the coming of the Prophet to the mosque when he was mortally sick.

A most sublime form of observance of the Sunnat is that even in human situations and intimate experiences of life one reacted within the limits of the Shariat. The Prophet felt sad on occasions of grief, and happy on occasions of joy, but some people imagine that the height of spirituality lies in supreme indifference to pain and pleasure, and a godly man should neither show signs of grief nor effects of joy at any time.

Hazrat Mujaddid Alf-Sani had taken exception to the conduct of a spiritual leader who had reminded unmoved when the news of the death of his son was communicated to him, and remarked that as the Prophet's son, Ibrahim, died, he was heard saying:

"There are tears in my eyes and grief in my heart, but I will say only what the Lord wants. Oh Ibrahim, I am sad at your death."

The Maulana would, perhaps, never had read it, but he wrote exactly the same to a friend who had suffered the loss of a child. He said:

"You have written to Yusuf, and it appears from your letter that you are altogether unaffected by the sad event. The Shariat does not permit it. To feel sad at thing of sorrow is natural, this, and Insha Allah, will, surely be your state, but it is, also, necessary to give expression to it. As you know well, it is essential to be affected by whatever circumstances the Lord may send, and to give expression to one's feelings in a proper way."

Similarly, he wrote to a deeply respected theologian on the birth of a child:

"It is a great favour of God on which one should be truly happy, and in case the joy is not felt in the heart, it should, at least, be expressed if only artificially."

Forbearance

Notwithstanding his highly sensitive nature, the Maulana was very tolerant and forbearing towards others. In a journey, a man who, also, happened to be educated, did all sorts of foolish things. The Maulana bore it patiently, and, in the end, he remarked, "Do you think my anger is so cheap that I will waste it on you? I shall not be provoked by you."

Once, as a *Tabligh* party returned from Gulaothi, it brought with it a young man about whom the members of the *Jama'at* complained that he never said Namaz and took delight in making fun of others. On seeing the Maulana, he immediately gave proof of it by bursting into laughter instead of paying respects. The Maulana, affectionately, touched his chin, and said, "May Allah always keep you in high spirits." He, then, counselled him in a most loving manner to observe. Namaz. The young man readily gave the assurance upon which people took him into the mosque.

Once, in a *Tabligh* congregation the Maulana unintentionally placed his hand on the shoulder of someone who flared up and said that he would hit the Maulana with his staff if he touched him again. The Maulana bent down, clasped his feet, and said, "You did not say about the feet. Did you?"

The Maulana was, once, travelling in a bullock-cart with a few companions. They were in a hurry to catch the bus and urged the Cartman to drive faster, but he did not listen and went on leisurely. When, on reaching the bus station, it was found that the bus had left, some members of the party began to scold the Cartman, but the Maulana simply said to him, "What harm was there if you had given heed to their request?"

Consideration for others

Innumerable instances are available of the Maulana's deep regard for the rights and sentiments of Muslims, particularly of men of learning and nobility. Whoever spent a few days with him would agree that it was one of his most endearing qualities. To a friend, he wrote:

"Always remember that love and respect for one another is more meritorious than anything else. To observe this one duty and to be steadfast in it is superior to and a surer means of earning the good pleasure of the Lord than upholding a thousand principles of the Shariat."

The Maulana, also, paid the fullest attention to the rights of mankind in general, including the polytheists and the infidels.

Once, a companion occupied more than his share of the space in a railway compartment. The Maulana reprimanded him.

"You have violated the right of fellowmen," he said. "The other passengers have a claim on the space you have occupied in excess of your need."

Once, the Maulana stopped the bus in which he was travelling in order to say the prayers, and after the Fard *Rak'ats* had been offered up, some of his companion formulated the intention for *Nafl Rak'ats*. The Maulana, thereupon, said, "Brothers, these other passengers, too, have a claim (on the bus)."

If, at a dinner party, people began to drink the meat- broth, the Maulana would stop them, saying, "It is a breach of faith. The host has not permitted it to you."

Once while going to Kandhla, the Maulana had to change from the third class to the second-class compartment owing to the rush of the passengers, thinking that he would have his ticket changed by the ticket-examiner when he came. The ticket-examiner came on his round, but his attitude was so provocative that the Maulana rebuked him. When he had gone, after changing the ticket, Maulana Inamul Hasan who was accompanying the Maulana told him that the ticket-examiner had the right to say what he did. The Maulana admitted his fault, and, at the next station, he got down and sought out the ticket-examiner and apologised to him.

Good manners

Conventional good manners that are related only to outward appearance are not scarce in the world, but once the condition of Iman and *Ihtisab* comes in and they are brought in line with the Sunnah and the Shariat, there will not be many who can lay a claim to them. The Maulana believed that there is no virtue in good manners if they are not brought under the feet of the sacred Prophet. He, often, related that when Sheikhul Hind Maulana Mahmood Hasan returned from Malta (where the British Government had imprisoned him), he was invited to a dinner at which the Maulana, also, was present. The host spoke highly of the politeness and gentility of a British officer. Maulana Mahmood Hasan listened patiently for some time, but when it went on and on, he said to the Maulana quietly, "Does an Infidel, too, have good manners?"

Those who had studied the Traditions, and, also, had an opportunity to observe the Maulana from close quarters, could easily appreciate the meticulous care he took to follow the example of the holy Prophet in everyday life. As I once wrote to the students of Nadwatul Ulema who were staying with the Maulana: "You have read the Traditions; now see how the Traditions are acted upon in social behaviour and monetary dealings."

The Maulana, once, wrote to a friend: "However lowly a Muslim may be, learn to look at him with respect." Even the most humble or defaulting Muslim was respectable in his eyes, and he seemed to regard him to be better and more beloved of God than himself. Whenever he met a Muslim, he thought only of the spark of Faith that lay within him, and all his faults and weaknesses faded before the reverence for Islam. He could easily know what was good and what was evil in a man and thought only of the aspect of goodness in him. Once, on meeting a person, he observed, "I know he has done great harm to a religious personality and a theological institution and it has hurt me very much, but I am, also, aware of his scholarship and it is to it alone that I have paid respect."

The Maulana had the greatest regard for the Ulema and wanted them to be held in high esteem. He would always have them sit at a place of honour, and if there was only a mat or carpet, he would spread a white sheet over it for them. There would come big Jama'ats from different places, and the Maulana would instinctively know to what ranks the visitors belonged and treat everyone according to his position. Very few people could complain that they had been ignored by the Maulana.

Hafiz Mohammad Husain (Ujrarwaley), who was an old gentleman and had been an attendant of Maulana Gangohi had come to visit the Maulana on hearing of his illness. He used to come into the Maulana's[1] apartment every day to do dam on him, and the Maulana's condition was that the slightest shaking of the cot hurt him. Thus, when people came to do the dam after the prayer-services, some attendants would stand near the cot to see that no one collided against it unknowingly. But the Maulana persuaded Hafiz Mohammad Husain to sit on his bed when he came in for dam in spite of his own discomfort and the silent disapproval of the attendants.

Once, the dining-mat had been near the tank and the Maulana's cot was placed out in the courtyard. Hafiz Saheb also, was, having the meal, but he was sitting a little removed from the main body of the diners. The Maulana, thereupon, sent word to Maulana Mohammad Zakaria to take him between himself and Maulana Abdul Qadir Raipuri.

---

[1] The blowing of air on the sick after reciting the prayers prescribed for the occasion.

The Maulana treated his colleagues and fellow- workers equally and did not like any distinction to be made among them whether they were staying with him at Nizamuddin or accompanying him on a journey. Once, at a night-halt during a tour, the cots were placed in such a way that the foot of the Maulana's cot was towards the head of the cot of a companion. The Maulana felt angry at it and took them to task who were responsible for the arrangement.

Once, a friend gathered the Maulana's shoes by way of reverence, while departing. The Maulana, quickly, took back the shoes and kissed the friend's hands. He would say that in the Traditions a great stress was laid on showing kindness to the guests."

It is related by Maulana Moinullah Nadwi that "once I was ill, and it was the month of Ramzan. As the food was being taken to me, the Maulana had stood up for *Nafl Rak'ats*. He told the boy who was carrying it to wait, but the boy did not seem to hear and brought the food upstairs where I was staying. On finishing the Namaz, the Maulana came to me and said, 'I had told the boy that I will take the food to you myself, but he did not understand. Then, he sat down near me and talked for a long time in a most affectionate manner."

The Maulana was an embodiment of humility. He did not like anyone to pay an undue respect to him. As he wrote to me: "I sincerely wish that you accepted my suggestion not to address my humble self by any other appellation besides my name. It would be a waste of words."

In the same way, he, once, wrote to Sheikhul Hadees Maulana Mohammad Zakaria who, in addition to being younger in age, was, also, his nephew and pupil:

"Your esteemed letter brought me joy and honour. I am eagerly looking forward to your visit. If, as you say, I am Hazrat[1], you are Hazratgar[2]. Who would have cared for a worthless person like me had you not paid attention to him and shown so much consideration? After Maulana Khalil Ahmad you were the first to entertain kindly feelings for me, and later on, Haji Sheikh Rasheed Ahmad, too, become favourably inclined. All this is, solely, owing to you people."

"Eager as I am for your visit, I fear that my fault will become more conspicuous in your presence. But I am sustained by the hope that in the company of men like you I may, also, be reformed to some extent."

The Maulana guarded himself strictly against complacency and never ceased to look inward. In fact, the more he grew in fame and popularity, the more attention did he pay to self-introspection. Often, he would request men of piety and enlightenment to keep a watch on him and tell frankly if they found a trace of vanity in his behaviour. For instance, he wrote to Maulana, Mohammad Zakaria and Hafiz Abdul Latif in September 1943:

"One thing about which I used to be very anxious before the month of Ramzan has receded into background owing to my physical and spiritual debility."

"It is that, by the grace of God, this work has advanced so much that seeing its ever-increasing popularity, I do not now feel secure against self and fear that I may easily fall a prey to conceit and vainglory. Hence, I am in dire need of supervision by godly men

---

[1] A title addressed to the great.

[2] Meaning maker of Hazrats.

like you and beg you to treat me as such by exhorting me to be steadfast in virtue and warning sternly against evil."

In the Ma'arif (Azamgarh) of November 1944, Allama Syed Sulaiman Nadwi writes:

"During the Maulana's stay in Lucknow, a friend gave a tea-party in his honour at the time of Asr. As there was no mosque in the neighbourhood, the Asr service was celebrated at the residence of the host. The Maulana gave the Azan, and told me to lead the service, but when I politely declined, he led the prayers himself. After the service, the Maulana turned back and facing the Muqtadis[1] said, 'Brother, I am caught in a trial and misfortune, and beg you to pray for me. Since I gave this call, people have begun to love me, and I fear that it makes me self-conceited, and I start thinking that I am a holy man. It is my constant prayer to the Lord to take me safely out of it and beg you, also, to join in the prayer."

Once, friends presented a costly carpet to the Maulana, which hung heavily on his mind. The Maulana gave an interesting speech on it and made a gift of it to a leading theologian of the town with the remark that "the gentleman gave it to me in the belief that I was a theologian, and now, I am relieving myself of it by presenting it to someone who, really, is a theological scholar."

The Maulana did not like the people to make way for him or show any other mark of esteem. Even during the tours of Mewat when he was the centre of attraction and thousands of persons came to see him, he made sure that no ceremonial welcome was accorded to him, or other unnecessary formalities observed.

---

[1] Signifying those offering Namaz behind the Imam.

When his condition had deteriorated, people were forbidden from shaking hands with him. One day, a stranger came who proceeded towards the Maulana's not to shake hands by jumping over the people. A Mewati attendant checked him with his hand upon which he got very angry and left the place in a hurry, cursing the Molvis. The Maulana admonished the attendant and said, "To hurt the feelings of a Muslims is most displeasing to God. Go and apologise to him and come back only when he has forgiven you." The attendant quietly went away to carry out the command and I myself saw that, outside the mosque, the stranger was hurling abuses and the poor Mewati was standing before him with folded hands and saying, "I have wounded your feelings and caused you pain. Forgive me either for the sake of God or after inflicting the penalty on me for my fault."

Magnanimity

Religious circles in India have, for a long time, been divided into narrow compartments, with each group imagining that it held the monopoly of knowledge and learning and no one outside it possessed any merit. It has become impossible to have relations even with persons belonging to the same group but having different political or other affiliations. The Maulana's case, however, was exceptional. He could easily accommodate warring religious groups and leaders. No Muslim was utterly devoid of virtue in his sight. There was some worth and merit in all of them. One group, he felt, should learn the trait or quality from the other for which it was distinguished. He wanted the *Tabligh* movement to enrich itself with the distinctive attributes of all groups and sections of the Muslims, and, also, knew how it was to be done.

Once I said to him, "The people of Nadwa have always held the religious and spiritual leaders in high regard, but have received no affection or sympathy in return. On the contrary, they have been treated as strangers. Thanks God that you treat us as your own people." The Maulana was deeply touched by it. "What are you saying?' He exclaimed. "Your group is a group of religious men while. I do not believe even in leaving the Aligarh people alone. It is not proper to keep them, also, at a distance."

It is for this reason that, in the *Tabligh* Movement, teachers and students of Mazahirul Uloom, Saharanpur, Darul Uloom, Deoband, Nadwatul Ulema, Lucknow, Jamia Millia, Delhi, and even of modern colleges and universities, and merchants, government servants and all other classes of Muslims are found working side by side, without any reservation or mistrust. The Maulana was generous in praise. If he admired one for devoutness, the other he regarded with respect for orderly conduct, wisdom or administrative ability. With all this, he firmly believed that all the talents of the Muslims should be pressed in the service of the Faith instead of being wasted on petty, trifling things. To a religious-minded merchant the Maulana wrote:

"I have been begging all friends and godly men like you to be my helpers. You should come forward to shoulder the responsibility in such a way that you became everything in it. Your courage, high-mindedness and wisdom demand that you took up. some living work."

Steadfastness

Firmness of purpose was yet another outstanding quality of the Maulana. It was, particularly, in evidence during the last day of his life when illness had reduced him to a mere skeleton, and he had grown so weak that his voice could be heard with difficulty even on placing the ear on his lips. In spite of extreme prostration, the Maulana did not offer a single Namaz without congregation during the whole period of his illness. When he had to interrupt the last Isha service of his life owing to the sudden call of nature, he, again, offered the prayers congregationally in his room.

Till about two months before his death, the wonderful spectacle was seen at all the five prayer times every day that though the Maulana did not have the strength to sit up in bed and needed the support of two men to stand in the row, as soon as the Azan was uttered the Maulana recovered enough vigour to carry out Ruku and Sujud and even the comparatively longer Qayam of Fajr with apparent ease, and, then, all the strength seemed to go away from him with Salaam[1], and he, again, had to be helped back to his cot.

When it had become altogether impossible for the Maulana to stand, he used to offer the prayers in congregation in the sitting posture, and when even that could not be done, he joined the service lying on his cot, which was placed at the end of the row.

Whether in a journey or staying at home, the Maulana was very particular about Azan, Iqamat[2] and *Jama'at*[3]. I have had numerous occasions of travelling with him by bus or train and I do not remember to have offered the prayers even once without them. However, overcrowded a railway compartment was, the Maulana

---

[1] Finishing salute by turning the face first to the right, then to the left.

[2] Denoting the second call to prayer which is uttered immediately before the commencement of a Fard Namaz.

[3] Congregation.

always gave the Azan, and, then, offered up. Namaz with Iqamat and *Jama'at*. Fellow- passengers, generally, made room for celebrating the service as the Azan was given and the Maulana offered the prayers in congregation with his colleagues.

Once I returned from a journey accompanied by a friend. who had not been able to offer up Namaz on the train owing to over-crowding. The first thing the Maulana enquired from us was whether we had said the prayers and felt greatly disappointed when I told him that while I had offered it up my friend had yet to do so. He remarked that he had not offered a single Namaz without congregation on the train since he had taken up the *Tabligh* work, which was about twenty years ago, so much so that Go had made it possible for him to observe the *Taraweeh* also on such occasions, though, sometimes, he could offer only two Rak'ats of it.

So far as the duty of sanctioning what was allowed and forbidding what was prohibited was concerned, the Maulana believed in gradation, but showed no leniency when it came to a thing that was clearly unlawful.

When the Maulana was proceeding on his last Haj, in 1939, there ensued a competition between two ships, one of which reduced the fare to fifty-five rupees, but its passengers had to take the inoculation from a lady which was not acceptable to the Maulana as she was a Naa- Mahram[1]. Friends urged him to hurry up and board the ship taking the inoculation from the lady otherwise he would have to pay Rs, 182/- instead of Rs. 55/- for each the tickets, but the Maulana was adamant, and the whole of the party stayed back.

---

[1] Meaning a woman who is not so closely related to a male that he cannot marry her in accordance with the Shariat.

Messages, thereupon, were exchanged with the authorities till the male doctor of the boat came fuming. "Where is the Molvi who will not take the inoculation from a lady doctor?" he angrily asked. The Maulana and his colleagues were, ultimately, inoculated by the male doctor and the tickets, too, were obtained at the rate of Rs. 55/- each. The Maulana observed that "no Naa- Mahram has yet touched my body. Only once did it happen that as I went to visit a lady who was critically ill, she tried to take my hands in her hands, but I quickly withdrew my hands, and only the tips of my fingers came into contact with her body."

Repentance, supplication, and remembrance of God

Repentance, supplication, and remembrance of God were the Maulana's life-breath, and, as he used to say, the pith and core of his Movement. He writes:

"The correct arrangement of our endeavour is that, in it, the work of heart must take precedence, i.e., the seeking of help from the Lord with self-abasement and humility and an-unwavering reliance upon His benevolence, and repentance by cutting oneself aloof from the world and all that is contained in it; the work of the limbs, i.e., physical toil and exertion for the things that are pleasing to God should come next, and, last of all, the work of the tongue, i.e., talking and. speech-making." In a letter to me, the Maulana said:

"It must always be remembered that the sole object of everything related to Faith is the development of the power of supplication. Greatest effort should, at all times, be made in that regard. If it may be possible that while the limbs are engaged in work, the power of the heart is directed towards. beseeching the Lord, try your best to attain that state."

In the same way, he wrote to Sheikhul Hadees Maulana Mohammad Zakaria:

"The purpose of writing these lines is to beg virtuous and high-minded men like you to pray to God humbly and in proportion to the gravity of the situation and your own station, and to persuade others, also, to do the same. It will be dangerous to give up or neglect the *Tabligh* endeavour, but, at the same time, I do not possess the strength to carry it forward at all. Our hope rests in God. He is the Best of Helpers."

The Maulana entreated the Lord with great fervour, and, sometimes, he got lost in it so completely as to become oblivious to what was going on around him. His entreaties, often, assumed the form of a speech. Among the prayers mentioned in the Traditions, the following remained on his lips more frequently:

"Our Lord: Our hearts and our forelocks and our limbs are all in Thy Hand. Thou hast not given us control over any of these, and when such is, the case, be our sole 'Protector and guide us along the Straight Path."

"O God: Treat us as is worthy of Thy Glory and not as we deserve. Easy is what Thou makest easy, and Thou makest easy even what is difficult when Thou willeth. There is no deity save Allah, the Most Gracious, the Dispenser of Grace.'

"O Thou, the Living, Eternal One! To Thy Mercy do I appeal. Correct all my states and hand me not. over to self for a moment for if Thou wilt hand me over to the self, thou wilt be handing me over to my weaknesses, sins and iniquities. Thou, alone, art the Forgiver of sins."

The Maulana had attained a state of absolute and unqualified reliance on God. There was nothing, however great or difficult, that was impossible in his sight. Once he told a colleague that he could establish a thousand Madrassas in Mewat if he felt sure that it would lead to correction and reform. He would provide the funds for a year, amounting to six Lakh rupees, within two days provided that he (the colleague) took the responsibility of running the Madrassas and left the Maulana alone to devote himself single-mindedly to the *Tabligh* work. The Maulana, latter on remarked that though he did not possess even six rupees at that time, he was confident that. when it was resolved sincerely to undertake a work of God, money would be found for it in no time."

Similarly, with utmost self-assurance he told a gentleman who wanted to donate some money for the cause that: 'I am sure if I will do the work of the Prophet's religion, God will fill this building (Darul Iqama) with gold and silver."

However, Maulana might be feeling tired in a journey, but he always had enough energy for *Nafl* prayers. He used to say, "my tiredness goes away with Namaz." On numerous occasions, was it seen that while the other people felt tired after ascending a hill and lay down for resting, the Maulana stood up for *Nafl* prayers and remained engaged in them for a long time, without showing a trace of fatigue.

Chapter VIII: Intellectual background of the *Tabligh* movement

Judged from the religious environment, in which Maulana Mohammad Ilyas had passed the early days of his life, it could hardly be imagined that the moral and spiritual state of the Muslims was rapidly on the decline. Since in those surroundings one, generally, came into contact with men of piety and spirituality, it was not unnatural to remain blissfully unaware of the real state of affairs. It was, thus, difficult for those who had been brought up in that atmosphere. to realise that there was anything else for them to do than to establish Maktabs and Madrassas, teach the Quran and the Sunnat, issue religious decrees, refute the innovations in Faith and attain self-purification through the path of *Tasawwuf*.[1]

The Maulana, too; could have settled for any of these courses and attained perfection in it through his extraordinary intelligence and ability, but God lent him His special guidance and it dawned upon him that the very foundations upon which the super-structure was to be raised were crumbling among the Muslims and even their belief in the fundamental articles of Faith was weakening day by day. In the Maulana's own words. "The fundamental doctrines have ceased to be fundamental and lost the power to sustain and regulate the subsidiary doctrines." Belief in the Godhead of God and in the Apostleship of the Prophet was steadily declining, the hereafter was losing its importance, and the dignity of the Word of God and the worth and significance of the sayings of the Apostle were getting reduced to meaningless terms.

[1] Islamic mysticism.

In a letter to Maulana Husain Ahmad Madni, the Maulana wrote:

"There is no limit to the ridicule and derision with which the very mention of things like Namaz, Roza, adherence to Faith and compliance with the Shariat is 'greeted among the Muslims. The basic aim of the *Tabligh* movement is the revival of the glory of these tenets and duties, and to bring about a change from scoffing to reverence."

Gross neglect

The Maulana had realised that the Muslims were drifting away from the elementary teachings of the Faith. To talk of the more advanced branches when the plant of Faith had yet to take root in the hearts was unreasonable and premature. What was the point in the establishment of new theological institutions when even the older ones were languishing and the veins and arteries, which carried blood to them, were getting harder and narrower day by day? No one was willing to acknowledge their need or to recall with gratitude the services of their founders, teachers, and other well-wishers. As the Maulana wrote to Haji Rasheed Ahmad, who was associated with a number of leading Madrassas:

"I had seen, fifteen years ago, the trend that was developing among the well-wishers, and felt that the way the Madrassas were functioning and being maintained, i.e., the interest and inclination of the people which led them to make donations and serve the institutions in various other ways was dwindling and it would soon disappear and there was not much hope for the future."

The Maulana had, also, felt that theological sciences were becoming unproductive, and, in fact, a burden on the pupils owing to the predominance of worldly interests. He said, "These sciences are becoming valueless because the aims and objects for which one acquired them have gone out of them and the ends and advantages for which these were studied are gained no longer. Keeping the two things in mind, I concentrated on this way, i.e., *Tabligh* of serving the Faith."

It was not that the Maulana did not consider the Maktabs and Madrassas essential for the Muslims. On the other hand, he regarded their extinction a curse and a misfortune. Writing to Haji Rasheed Ahmad on the closing down of a large number of Madrassas in Mewat, he said:

"You must emphasise that the stagnation or closure of hundreds of Madrassas is a source of great misfortune for the people and there is the danger of our being called to account on the Day of Final Judgement that the Quran was disappearing from the world and there was no share in our wealth and no anxiety in our hearts for it."

The Madrassas had been founded upon the ground our ancestors had prepared, and deep anxiety for the preservation and propagation of Islam had induced religious-minded Muslims to set them up so that the younger generations did not remain ignorant of Faith. It was on account of this awareness and solicitude, however weak, that the Madrassas were functioning and getting pupils. But the stock of eagerness and earnestness was running out fast which was a most alarming portent for the future of Faith and the survival of the Madrassas.

The Primary need, therefore, was to revive the ardour and enthusiasm among the Muslims. It should be brought home to them that there was no other way to acquire Faith than to learn it, and the learning of Faith was more important than the learning of material arts and sciences. Once this realisation was produced, the rest would be easy. The general ailment of the Muslims was lethargy and listlessness. It had been presumed that Faith was present among them, and hence attention was being diverted towards things of a secondary nature.

A notable change that had come over religious preaching, instruction, and reform, as compared to the earlier times, was that it had got restricted to seekers, and nothing was being done for those who were the victims of complacency and oblivious to the need for improvement. The world was sunk in torpor whenever the Apostles were raised up. They aroused it from deep slumber, produced earnest seekers of truth, and trained men for their mission. To stimulate the mindless and apathetic people and to enkindle the desire for correction and change in their hearts was the real end and purpose of *Tabligh.*

Method

But how was it to be done? The Kalima of *Laa ilaah* was the end of the Rope of Allah which was in the hands of every Muslim. By seizing that end you can pull him towards the whole Faith. He cannot resist it. As long as the Muslim affirms the Kalima, there will be a good chance of bringing him over to Faith. The opportunity must be seized with both hands before it is lost altogether.

The only way now to create religious consciousness among the Muslims was that contact was made with them through the Kalima. It should be taught to them if they did not know it already and seen that they pronounced it correctly. Its significance should be explained to them, and they should be told what the affirmation of servility to God and loyalty to the Prophet meant. They should be roused and brought round to observing the duties to God and the Apostle, the foremost among which was Namaz. God had endowed Namaz with the exceptional quality of generating the strength and ability to adhere and be faithful to the whole of Faith. It was the primary and most manifest evidence of loyalty and obeisance avowed through the Kalima. For further advancement and solidity, the Muslims were to be exhorted to remember the Lord much and often, and it should exhort to remember the Lord much and often, and it should be made clear to them that for living as Muslims it was necessary to acquire knowledge of the will and purpose and commands and injunctions of God. No art or skill could be acquired without spending some time over it. The same was true of Faith. One had to find time for it, aside of one's pre- occupations. The task was so extensive that it was beyond the capacity of a few individuals or groups. The general body of the Muslims must come forward to fulfil it. In the words of the Maulana: "If Lakhs will not rise up for the sake of crores, how will it be done? There are not as many Lakhs who know as crores who do not."

For it, the Maulana was convinced that a ceaseless and universal endeavour had to be launched in the whole of the Muslim World. Action and movement were a permanent and intrinsic part of the life of a Muslim. Lethargy and preoccupation with worldly affairs were a passing phenomenon. The foundation of the Muslim millet was laid on struggle and endeavour for Faith. It was for it that it had been raised up otherwise there was nothing lacking in any sphere of worldly activity to remove which a new community had to be brought forth. The decline of the Muslims began when they neglected this duty and grew spiritually weak and listless, and their habits became sedentary, and they acquired fondness for the softer ways of urban life. It started with the end of the Glorious Caliphate. Says the Maulana:

"We stopped setting out in batches in the path of Faith although it was a fundamental duty. The Prophet himself used to go from place to place and whoever took the pledge at his hand, also, began to do the same as a man possessed. When, in Mecca, Islam was confined to the individual plane, everyone who became a Muslim strove individually to preach the Faith to others. In Madina, there was a more civilised and collective life. On migrating to it, the prophet started sending out parties in all directions, and as the Muslims grew in number, they acquired a martial character. Peaceful life was possible only to those who served as the refuge and sustainers of the wanderers. To be in a state of movement and active endeavour in the path of Faith was the thing the mattered. When it ceased, the Caliphate, too, came to an end."

Design of work

The plan of work, in the Maulana s own words, was as follows:

"The real *Tabligh* is of two things, and the rest consists only of giving it a definite shape. One of these things is material and the other is spiritual. By 'material' we mean what is related to the limbs, i.e., revival of the practice of travelling in batches from place to place and country to country for the propagation of the Guidance brought by the Prophet, while the 'spiritual' half denotes the engendering of sentiments, i.e., giving rise, once again, to the custom of laying down one's life at the command of God, as has been set forth in the Quran:

"By nay, by thy Lord, they will not believe (in truth) until they make thee judge of what is in dispute between them and find within themselves no dislike of that which thou decide and submit with full submission. (IV: 65)

"I created the Jinn and humankind only that they might worship Me. (LI: 86)

1. To strive for the things brought by the sacred Prophet in proportion, to their importance. As, unfortunately, we are getting unacquainted with the Kalima, its preaching should receive paramount attention, which, in truth, lies in the affirmation of the godhead of God, i.e., our sole ambition should be to lay down our lives at the behest of Allah.
2. To pay attention, after the correction of the Kalima, to the correction of Namaz and ending it with as much likeness to the Namaz of the holy prophet as possible.
3. To engage, in morning and evening and in some part of the night, in gaining the knowledge of Faith and remembrance of God.
4. To travel in order to spread the teachings of the Prophet in all parts of the world.
5. To train oneself in good moral and social behaviour during the travels and to fulfil the duties of God and fellowmen with sincerity.
6. (Correction of intention), i.e., to seek Diving good pleasure and betterment of life in the Hereafter through carrying out the Commands of God with fullest faith in the promises made by Him on each Command.

A great evil, which is the source of a thousand evils these days and has deprived the Muslims of each-other's virtues and Islam of the collective goodness of the Muslims, is the disparagement of fellow Muslims. Every Muslim has taken it for granted that he is the embodiment of virtue while all the other Muslims are mean, vicious and sinful, and, hence, he, alone, is worthy of esteem. This attitude is responsible for all the ills and evils that are plaguing the religious and social life of the Muslims.

There was a special favour of the Lord on Maulana Mohammad Ilyas in this regard, and he made respect for Muslims a cardinal point of his endeavour. The nature of the *Tabligh* movement is such that, in it, one has to deal with all sorts of Muslims, and numerous difficulties can arise if this basic principle is overlooked.

In place of the prevalent attitude of self-righteousness, the Maulana insisted that people saw their own faults and learnt to admire the good qualities of others. It was the only way to ensure peace and co-operation in individual as well as collective life.

As the Maulana, once, wrote:

"There is no man or Muslim who is wholly good or wholly bad. Everyone has his own virtues and weaknesses. If the practice of appreciating the good and ignoring the bad points of each other became current, among us, many evils will disappear, by themselves, from the work, and virtues will take their place. But unfortunately, what obtain in actual practice, today, is far different."

By his own example and through instruction and exhortation the Maulana had instilled into the Mewatis and other *Tabligh* workers reverence for the Kalima and respect for the Muslims so well that it had become a part of their nature. Together with it, the emphasis on Zikr and Ilm[1], and on abstention from vain and fruitless conversation, and rendering obedience to the leader, and working

---

[1] Denoting knowledge. Here it signifies the gaining of the knowledge of Faith.

as a united body, in accordance with the rules, had made the Movement safe against the sad experiences that, generally, befell those who are associated with the work of religious reform and instruction.

Preparing the ground

According to the Maulana, the Faith was the soil and to travel from place to place for its propagation among the masses was like the preparation of the soil, while theological institutions and other manifestations of the religious life of the Muslims could be compared to the orchards, and, naturally, the more fertile and well-irrigated the soil, the more flourishing would be the orchards. The primary need, therefore, was to prepare the soil and make it fertile. As he writes:

"Striving in the cause of *Tabligh* and going from place.to place is, for theological institutions and all other religious affairs, like preparing the soil, and the other religious activities are like planting trees on it. Groves are of many kinds. There are groves of dates, apples, pomegranates, bananas, and so on. But no grove can be grown without hard work in two directions. One is the preparation of the soil, without which nothing can be done, and the other is taking care of the trees. The *Tabligh* movement, thus, is the soil of the Faith, and the institutions are the groves. So far, the soil of the Faith has been lying neglected.

How, then, can trees be grown on it?"

And again:

How can a community whose degeneration has gone so far that it has sunk even below the words of the Kalima of *Laa Illaah illallah* be reformed at the top without starting from the bottom. The end cannot be corrected without the correction of the beginning. If it is corrected at the starting point and set on the right course, it will reach the top by itself, while to hope for reformation at the top when the base is unsound is pure illusion."

The Maulana, thus, regarded his Movement essential for the preservation of Faith and believed no effort or sacrifice to be too much for it. He said:

"I cannot think of any other way to the progress and advancement of our Movement, the need of which is accepted on all hands, than that everyone got ready to sacrifice whatever he had.

"Like Jehad, it, too, in its typical form, is a foremost religious duty, and it is binding on all Muslims to take an active interest in it. Doubtlessly, among all the efforts that are being made today, it is nearest to the method of the holy Prophet."

In a talk with Maulana Ataullah Shah Bukhari, during his last illness, the "Maulana explained his viewpoint in these words:

"In the beginning, when I taught in the Madrassas, a large number of pupils came to study, and there were many good and promising boys among them. I thought that the net result of the time and energy I spent on them could only be that after graduating from the Madrassa, they would become Molvis[1] and Alims[2], and then, take to professions that were, generally, accepted during those days. Some of them would learn the Unani system of medicine and open their clinics, some would pass the university examinations and become teachers in schools and colleges, and some would have to

---

[1] Meaning theological scholars.

[2] Meaning theological scholars.

rest content with serving as Molvis in the Madrassas. That was all. I, thereupon, lost interest in teaching in the Madrassa.

"Then a time came when my spiritual mentor gave me the permission to teach Zikr to the seekers of Truth, and I, also, felt inclined towards it. By the grace of God, those under my instruction made such a rapid progress that even I was surprised. With it, I, also, started thinking what it all was and where would it lead to. At the most, some men of spiritual merit would be produced, and people would come to them with requests to invoke Divine favour on their behalf to win a lawsuit or give them an amulet for having children. It could, also, be that the chain of guidance and instruction endured for some time because of them.

Ultimately, I lost interest in it as well, and resolved that the proper use of the capabilities God had endowed me with was that those were employed for the same purpose for which the holy Prophet had employed his own capabilities, i.e., for leading the bondmen of the Lord, specially the heedless and the negligent, towards Him and giving rise to the practice of striving to the utmost, even to the extent of sacrificing one's life for the glory of the Word of God. This, solely, is our endeavour, and this is all that I say to everyone. If this work is seriously undertaken, a thousand times more Madrassas and Sufi-lodges will get established automatically, or, rather, every Muslim will become a Madrassa and a Khanqah[1] and the boon and blessing brought by the sacred Prophet will come to be distributed at the level of the common man."

To a friend asking for an amulet, the Maulana wrote:

[1] Meaning an abode of holy men: a Sufi-hospice.

"May God bless you, brother, I possess no knowledge of the amulets, charms and incantations. It will, however, be most beneficial if you learnt *Tabligh* from me for steadfastness in Faith. It will make the life of this world easy and the life of Futurity pleasant for you. I want to devote all my time to *Tabligh* though I know it not as well."

Similarly, in another letter, he said:

"I know nothing of amulets and charms. For me, the panacea for all the ills and evils is *Tabligh*. God is pleased with the ascendancy of Faith, and cool comfort is brought to the Prophet in his mausoleum. Thus, God will mend everything by Himself when His good pleasure will be sought, and comfort brought to the sacred Prophet."

In yet another letter, the Maulana wrote:

"My friend, I am neither a conjurer nor a soothsayer I, also, know nothing about charms and amulets. I am an ignorant man lying in the corner of a mosque. By the grace of God, I strive for the correction of the life of Futurity, and my sole anxiety is that God made me of those who derive benefit from the holy Prophet. This is my one and only occupation. If you and your friends are in need of it, pay heed to what I say. Maybe, it does you some good."

Tending to the roots of the Faith

The Maulana had realised that the leaves and branches of the tree of Faith were withering because its roots had dried up. The freshness and radiance of supererogatory deeds was diminishing owing to the neglect of fundamental duties. Says he:

"The supererogatory acts of worship, prayer-formulas, entreaties and supplications, in fact, everything in the line of religion are the leaves and flowers of Faith. Now, how can the leaves and flowers of a tree preserve their freshness when it has dried up at the root? That is why, in my humble opinion, neither the prayer-formulas are being effective these days, nor supplications, nor the spiritual attention and inclination of anyone. As a Tradition has it, 'When the endeavour for the preaching and propagation of Faith, which consists of sanctioning what is right and forbidding what is wrong, will have ceased, the prayers of the devotees who spend their nights in crying to the Lord and their supplication avail nothing. 'The Gates of Mercy have been closed. It is futile to hope for improvement in the condition of the Muslims until they make efforts for the preservation and propagation of Islam." It is the Will of God that He will turn with mercy towards the Muslims only when they strive for the glory of Faith and spend their time and energy on it."

To feel earnestly for Faith was an essential attribute of a Muslim. There was, he said, a great danger of being put to humiliation and disgrace in the Hereafter for the Believer who remains indifferent to the Call of *Tabligh* and does not participate in the endeavour for the revival and regeneration of Faith.

"Believe me", says the Maulana in a letter, "Whoever dies without grief in his heart over the extinction of Islam dies the worst kind of death. On the Day of Resurrection, he will rise with a blackened face."

In the same way, on the occasion of a *Tabligh* meeting in Mewat, he wrote:

"Give glad tidings to those who worked towards the success of the meeting. Tell them that as they have striven to change the scene of mutual discord and hatred into that of the glory of the Word of God, this act of theirs shall Insha Allah, be mentioned, on the Day of Final Requital, from the pulpit where all the men and Jinn and angels and Apostles will be present."

Change of outlook is essential for reform.

The religious surroundings in which the Maulana had been brought up did not permit of any laxity or hesitation in the forbidding of what was wrong and sanctioning of what was right in the eye of the Shariat. In fact, it was owing to this constancy and resoluteness that many lawful things were made current in the religious circle to which he belonged, and unlawful things were eradicated, and numerous defunct Sunnats were revived.

The Maulana knew that the way to remove the evils was not to grapple with them one by one for often a lifetime was spent in uprooting a sinful practice, and, yet, no progress was made, and even if some success was gained, it remained confined to a particular class or group, and, sometimes, it, also, happened that if one evil was eradicated, another took its place. It would, thus, take centuries of struggle to rid the world of the innumerable vices and iniquities that were prevalent in it. The wisest course would be to avoid a direct assault on them and concentrate on the promotion of religious conscience and giving rise to lawful and virtuous acts and practices.

The Maulana did not believe in piecemeal reform. He would say, "Come from far and near, changing the environment all the way and spreading what is good and lawful. The evil and forbidden things will disappear by themselves. The more the positive virtues and legitimate acts will flourish, the more will the moral and religious faults and sinful deeds and habits lose their hold and pass from existence."

It was related to me by a Mewati that, once, he was wetting the ground with water to make it cool. He poured the water all around him, but the place where he was standing remained dry, and then, a cool breeze came and the temperature of that place, also, fell down. At that time, he realised that if he had poured water only where he was standing and the surrounding ground had remained dry, it, too, would not have become cool, and, it was with it, that the wisdom of the Maulana's method dawned upon him.

About a village which was devoid of religious feeling, the Maulana wrote:

"It would not be correct to make a direct approach. A better course would be to persuade the people of the adjoining village to take *Tabligh* parties to it. They should first be brought into a proper frame of mind, and it is only then that a direct appeal can bear fruit, otherwise the consequences will be even more disastrous.

"A man is always influenced by his environment. This is the guiding principle of our Movement. It is most difficult to take a man out of his surroundings. The aim should, therefore, be to change the surroundings."

The Maulana insisted that the whole life should be brought under the influence of Faith.

"Keep your spirits high in the service of Faith", said he to a friend. "You cannot imagine how much joy will it bring to the soul of the sacred Prophet, and God willing, you will see a marvellous improvement."

Similarly, to a friend who was, probably, interested in the religious uplift of the trading classes, the Maulana wrote:

"In my humble view, the ultimate purpose of *Tabligh* to which I invited you and for which I am, also, striving to the best of my ability is to bring the trade, commerce and agriculture of the Muslims under the control of the Shariat. The starting point of *Tabligh* is worship, and without the perfection of worship, no progress can be made towards the observance of the teachings of Islam in social conduct and monetary dealings. The primary object of the earnest bondmen should, therefore, be the propagation and perfection of the A.B.C. of *Tabligh*, i.e., worship in the world. Moral conduct, social behaviour and monetary dealings can be reformed only through it."

Popular method of *Zikr* and *Ta'allum*

Maulana Mohammad Ilyas gave a general call of *Zikr* and *Ta'allum*[1] to the Muslims, but in his scheme of things, these terms possessed a special significance. Throughout India, or, rather, the Islamic World, there are in vogue some definite prayer-formulas for *Zikr* and a special course of study are prescribed for the Madrassas. Gradually, *Zikr* and *Ta'aullum* have become so institutionalised that to observe or pursue them outside the traditional design is considered inconceivable. The Maulana held a revolutionary idea in these matters as well. He felt that while the established order was necessary, only a few persons could profit by it. The general body of Muslims could make little or no progress in *Zikr* and knowledge within a limited period of time.

---

[1] Meaning learning knowledge: study.

After a deep study of the life-record of the holy companions, the Maulana had concluded that the method. which was followed during the early phase of Islam, was the most natural way for the education and instruction of the Ummat. About *Zikr* he felt that it would be a grave folly to neglect it, yet, at the same time, he was sure that it should not be confined to the repetition of a few sets prayer-formulas. To bear in mind the rules and principles laid down for various walks and circumstances of life and to abide by them at each step was the sum and essence of God- remembrance, and the main task lay in reviving, in Ummat, the spirit of Iman and Ihtisab. All the same, it was, also, necessary to include vocal *Zikr* in the plan of *Tabligh*. He wrote:

"Believing *Tabligh* to be an easy and unfailing means of seeking the countenance of the Lord, keep yourselves engage in this task, carrying out Zikr much and often and making earnest entreaties to Him, with the head bent low in genuflexion. Tell others, also, to do the same. Remembrance of God and supplication are the essence of *Tabligh*.

As for education, the Maulana believed that to confine it to books and Madrassas was to exclude a large section of the Ummat from acquiring it. Only a small minority of Muslims would be able to profit by it, and that, too, only intellectually. The direct method through which the masses could acquire not only religious knowledge but, also, realise its inner reality without the usual paraphernalia was that of personal contact, association and congregation and active participation in religious effort and coming out of one's traditional environment. Just as language and good manners were learnt best in the company of men of culture and education, in the same way correct knowledge of religion was acquired in the company of and close association with men of Faith and piety. Faith was a living and dynamic thing while books were lifeless and devoid of feeling and spirit, and to obtain the animate from the inanimate was contrary to the law of nature. A part of the Faith was related to the limbs, and it could be acquired only by moving the limbs, and a part of it was related to the heart, which could be transmitted only from one heart to another, and a part it was related to mind, and this could be gained, of course, by reading the books. As he said:

"Every limb of a man has a function to perform. The eye is meant for seeing and it must do that. It cannot be used for hearing. In the same way, it is the function of the heart to react to the surroundings, and the mind gives a definite form to what the heart feels. Mind is governed by the heart, and feeling is produced in the heart by the external environment, and the giving of form to it is called knowledge. The mind will form the correct image, i.e., acquire knowledge, only when the response of the heart is correct, and this is not possible through the books. It can be produced only by action. I do not say that the Madrassas should be closed down. The Madrassas are for the perfection of education, but they are not suited for the elementary stage."

Another thing needed for the advancement of education was share with others the knowledge one had acquired. To put it in Maulana's own words:

"Know that a scholar cannot make progress in learning until he imparts what he has learnt to those who are inferior to him in knowledge, particularly to those who are on the borderline of Apostasy."

To acquire religious knowledge and to develop true religiousness was an essential component of the life of a Muslim. Merely to earn and spend and remain negligent towards the Faith was not worthy of him. Similarly, a Muslim's life cannot be altogether devoid of the urge and effort for the propagation and preservation of Faith. There must be some place for it. The lives of the holy Companions were, generally, marked by four things: learning, *Zikr*, *Tabligh,* and earning of livelihood. But now, livelihood has swept aside the other three things and left no room for any other idea or activity.

But the answer did not lie in calling upon the people to give up their worldly occupations for the sake of the neglected tasks. The wisest thing was to work for the revival of the way of life of the Companions. Instead of demanding from the people to abandon the worldly interests, they should be induced to find time for Faith in the midst of them and make the best use of it by spending it in the company of the seekers of religious knowledge and men of Faith.

Faith ought not to be studied in parts, but as a whole. Not only the rules and proprieties of worship and other obligatory duties, but the rules and regulations prescribed in the Shariat concerning social behaviour, moral conduct, monetary dealings, companionship, and eating and drinking, too, should be learnt and acted upon. Together with it, religious spirit needs, also, be cultivated.

The Maulana had got together all these things in his programme of the *Tabligh* tours. He wanted this way of gaining the higher advantages of religious instruction. without the Madrassas and the money and organisation needed for them, by millions of Muslims who were engaged in various occupations to be introduced and made current in the Ummat. "If this way of life becomes common", he said, "and this path is opened even at the cost of laying down our lives, it would be possible for the busiest people in the Ummat to avail themselves of religious instruction and guidance."

Moreover, along with religious knowledge, a man, also, gains in general understanding and matureness by living religion the practical way, and dealing with different people, and keeping regular company with men of Faith during the tours. It would be difficult for those who never had a personal experience of *Tabligh* tours to appreciate their significance. The following extracts from the letter of a University graduate will give some idea of the educative value of the tours. The names of persons occurring in it have, deliberately, been omitted:

"The *Jama'at* left for Kharagpur at 3 p.m., on Saturday, the 4th of November Was appointed as the leader of the *Jama'at*. It consisted of 32 persons who were the representatives of all the Zonal *Jama'ats* except one. Ten of them had already been on *Tabligh* tours while for the rest it was the first experience of its kind.

"Kharagpur is 72 miles from Calcutta. To find accommodation, without any difficulty, for the whole of the party in a third-class compartment, and that, too, on Bombay Mail (during war-time) was due, simply, to the propitiousness of the *Tabligh* movement."

"Was reached Kharagpur a little before the Maghrib prayers. The prayers were offered up in congregation on the platform. After it, the *Jama'at* left for the town. We made the usual prayer before entering the town. Permission for stay at the Jam'i Masjid had already been obtained from the Chairman of the Managing Committee. Was in charge of meals. We ate together. After the Isha service, the aims and objects of *Tabligh* were explained in a brief speech which lasted for about 15 minutes, and an appeal was made to those present to go on the round with the *Jama'at*. The *Jama'at* listened to the reading out of a few pages from Hayat-i-Sahaba (Lives of the Companions) before retiring to bed.

"Most of us offered the Tahajjud prayers. We had the breakfast together after the Ishraq prayers, and the daily routine of Zikr etc., was, also, completed. The session of instruction went on uninterruptedly till 12:30 p.m. At first, an article by Maulana Mohammad Manzoor Nomani was read out, which had appeared in Al-Furqan of Lucknow and contained necessary guidance regarding the work of *Tabligh*, and, then a part of Hayat-i-Sahaha. With us was a Qaari[1] of who had everyone recite Surat-i-Fateha, to him, turn by turn, and corrected the mistakes. After it, the rules and proprieties of *Wuzu* were taught from a book on Fiqh[2], and, then, the six principles of *Tabligh* were narrated by some members of the party, which was followed by a discussion. After it, I and the leader of the *Jama'at* gave an account of the tours of Delhi and Mewat. All this took about 4½ hours, and the mealtime had arrived when the programme ended.

"The Zuhr service was celebrated after the meal. By that time, a fairly large number of persons had assembled to whom I explained the guidelines of door-to-door approach, and the *Jama'at* left on the round 1, the leader of the *Jama'at*, and were to act as the spokesmen. Many local people, also, had joined the party. The *Tabligh* was very successful, and the Muslims everywhere listened to us attentively. Our round took us to another mohalla[3] where we offered the Asr prayers in the mosque, and, after the service, people were told briefly of the revolution that had come over Mewat. With the co-operation of the Imam of the mosque a *Jama'at* was formed, and we returned, with the new *Jama'at*, to Jam'i Masjid by the time of the Maghrib prayers, showing to it, in the way, how the work of Tabligh

---

[1] One who is skilled in the recitation of the Quran.

[2] Islamic Jurisprudence.

[3] Meaning a quarter or part of a town.

was actually done. The congregation at Maghrib was very large and it was heartening to see that the people to whom the appeal was made during the round had come to begin a new life, after taking a bath and putting on a clean dress.

"The Amir asked me to speak after the service. I do not exactly remember what I said, but, by the grace of God, it made an impact on the audience, and the response was enthusiastic. Twenty-five persons spontaneously enrolled themselves for the *Jama'at.* including the President of the Managing Committee of the mosque who was selected as the leader of the *Jama'at.*

"As ......is here these days, he was appointed to guide the activities of the *Jama'at* along the right lines. Visitors continued to come long after the congregation.

"After dinner, the party left for the railway station on foot with everyone carrying his luggage on his shoulders. On reaching the station, we lay down to rest. The train arrived at 12.30 p.m., and even in those days of heavy rush on the trains a compartment was found which could accommodate the whole of the party and enough space was still left for four or five of the younger colleagues to lie down and sleep. The Fajr prayers were offered in the compartment. "We arrived back at 7.45 a.m. on Monday and after the prayers at the railway station, we embraced each-other (as an expression of goodwill) and left for our homes."

Summing up his impressions of the tour, the writer says:

i) fulfilled his responsibilities as the Amir so well that we all felt very happy over it. I have not found the Amir of any *Jama'at* more efficient and considerate. He looked after everyone's comfort throughout the journey, carried the luggage of others on his shoulders. in addition to his own, in spite of old age, filled the glasses with water at mealtimes and refrained from sitting down to eat until everybody had been seated comfortably, helped others to perform Wuzu on the train and drew their attention to its rules and proprieties, kept watch while the others slept and exhorted the members of the party to remember God much and often. and did all this most willingly. For a person who was superior to all of us in age. social status and wealth to behave as the servant of everyone was the most unforgettable experience of the tour.

ii) "After the Amir. the man to impress us most was He arranged for our meals, railway tickets etc. in an admirable manner. He paid for everything himself and. at the end of the journey, presented to every one of us an account of the expenses and accepted the payment."

iii) "Members of the party who had not undertaken a *Tabligh* tour earlier said with one voice that those were the best days of their lives."

The *Tabligh* endeavour is ideally suited to meet the demands of time and repel the mounting challenge of irreligiousness. The present-day Materialists make a direct appeal to the masses and sedulously sow the seeds of doubt and disbelief among them. They are a dedicated and resourceful people who know how to sell their ideas. Ideological combats, religious literature and plans and activities that are confined to the elite and do not involve the common man cannot arrest the progress of Apostasy and Materialism. Only a religious movement which begins at the grassroots and goes straight to the farmer's cottage and the artisan's workshop and ignores no section of the society can provide an effective answer to the menace of irreligiousness.

Chapter IX: Sayings of the Maulana

(As we have seen in the Introduction, Maulana Mohammad Manzoor Nomani used to note down the utterances of Maulana Mohammad Ilyas, bearing a special significance to the Tabligh movement. With the Maulana's permission, he had, also, begun to publish them in his monthly journal, Al-Furqan, of Lucknow. After the death of the Maulana, a collection of these reports, running into about 200 pages, was brought out which constitutes a valuable source for the Urdu-knowing people of obtaining an idea of the religious distinctiveness of Maulana Mohammad Ilyas and of his call and viewpoint, and the passionate burning of his heart for the propagation and preservation of the Faith.

Now that this English edition of *Maulana Mohammad Ilyas Aur Un ki Deeni Dawat* is being produced, it has been found advisable to add a few pages, containing 42 of his sayings, to it. It is hoped that the worth and usefulness of the book will be enhanced by the addition).

(i) The Maulana said: "The condition of the followers the Prophet has, generally, been that as the distance between them and the period during which the Prophet they followed lived increased, religious duties like worship lost their inner content and were reduced to mere rituals. For the correction of this fault and deficiency, new Apostles were raised up who put an end to this state of affairs and made the people appreciate the fundamental nature of the religious practices and the true spirit of the Shariat. When the Last of the Apostles, the Prophet

Mohammad, was raised up, the condition of the peoples who were the adherents of a Divine faith was similar, and the part of the Shariat brought by their Prophet that was still with them, also, had turned into a collection of a few soulless formalities. They regarded these ceremonies to be the real faith and canonical law. The holy Prophet brought these rituals to an end and taught authentic religious truths and commandments.

"Now, the Muslims, too, have fallen a prey to the same malady and even their modes of worship have, basically, degenerated into empty rituals, and what is more, theological education, which should have been the means of correction, has, at many places, become a formality.

"But since the order of the Apostles has ended and the responsibility for such thing has now devolved on the Ulema who are the deputies of the sacred Prophet, it is their duty to pay a special attention to the correction of this state, and the way to it is the rectification of 'Intention'; for ritualism enters into religious duties only when the spirit of sincerity and humbleness goes out of them, and by the correction of 'Intention' the direction of the deeds is set right, and 'reality' is produced in them in place of 'formalism', and, then, every deed is performed in the spirit of servility and godliness. In brief, it is the special responsibility of the Ulema and other religious persons, at the present time, to strive for the promotion of earnestness and 'reality' in the deeds of the people by drawing their attention to the correction of 'Intention'.

ii) The Maulana said: "It has been stressed over and over again in the Quran and the Traditions about Faith that it is Yusr. i.e., there is no hardship in it. It is easy, and capable of being observed by everyone. A thing should, thus, be easy in proportion to its importance in Faith. Now, since the correction of 'Intention' and single minded devotion to God is most important, and, in fact, the essential factor of all religious deeds and action, it also is the easiest part of the faith, and since single minded devotion to God is the sum and essence of Sulook, it follows that Sulook, too, is easy. But it must, also, be borne in mind that a thing is easy only when it is performed according to the prescribed method otherwise even the easiest thing becomes difficult. Where the people err is that they have presumed that it is very difficult to abide by the precepts and regulations though even the most ordinary things do not get done until the rules are observed and the correct way of doing them is followed. The ship, the motor car, the railway train-all function according to a fixed principle, and some method has to be followed even in cooking."

iii) The Maulana said: "The place of obligatory duties is much higher than that of supererogatory ones. In fact, the very purpose of supererogatory duties is to bring the obligatory duties to perfection or make amends for the deficiency that may have remained in them. Thus, the obligatory duties are the real thing, and the supererogatory deeds are secondary. But the case with some people is that they neglect the obligatory duties and pay much greater attention to supererogatory acts. For instance, as you all know, the 'invitation to goodness' and the 'sanctioning of what is allowed' and 'forbidding of what is prohibited', (in brief, all the branches of *Tabligh*), are among the more important obligatory duties, but how many people fulfil them while the number of those who carry out supererogatory acts of God-remembrance is much greater."

iv) The Maulana said: "When a bondsman of the Lord seeks to advance towards a virtuous act, Satan opposes him in various ways and puts all sorts of obstacles in his path. But if the bondsman remains unaffected and goes ahead, the Devil changes his tactics and tries to impair the sincerity of his act and wholesomeness of his 'Intention'. Sometimes, his attempt is to put into the doer's heart the desire for fame or ostentation, and, sometimes, he wants to ruin the purity of the act by other means. Religious workers should, therefore, always be on their guard against such deceptions and keep a constant watch on their 'Intention' for as soon as any other desire or motive save the seeking of the good pleasure of God gets mixed up with an act, it ceases to be acceptable to Him."

v) The Maulana said: "The foremost requirement of religious education is that a man looked into himself and understood his faults and shortcomings and did his bests to observe his duties. On the other hand, if he uses his knowledge and understanding to scrutinise the deeds of others and count their failings, it is intellectual vanity which is highly ruinous for men of learning and scholarship."

vi) The Maulana said, "A person feels relief on attaining a thing he desires. For instance, if a person is fond of luxurious living, good food and expensive clothes, he cannot be happy without them, while if he likes to sit on a mat and eat simple food and wear a plain dress, he will feel comfortable only when he has these things. Hence, there is a great favour of the Lord on those who, in emulation of the example of the holy Prophet, prefer to lead a plain and simple life, and feel grateful to the Lord for giving them the will and inclination to derive joy and comfort from things that are inexpensive and within the reach of everyone. They would, probably, have felt uneasy and discontented all their lives had God made them fond of costly things which only the rich could afford."

vii) The Maulana said: "Real Zikr is that in whatever profession, state or circumstances a man may be, he should do his best to observe the commands of God that are intended for such a situation, and it is this Zikr that I urge upon my friends."

viii) The Maulana said: "The tongue plays the most important part in the superiority man enjoys over all other created beings. If a person utters only good things with his tongue and uses it only for a worthy and virtuous purpose, his superiority will be based upon goodness, while if he uses his tongue as an instrument of mischief. as for instance, indulges in evil talk and causes hurt to others, his superiority will be based on wickedness so much so that, sometimes, it will make him worse than a dog or swine. As it is stated in a Tradition 'Men will be cast headlong into Hell on account of their vain and foolish talk."

ix) The Maulana said, "People attach even lesser importance to obedience to God than to obedience to men. Slaves and servants, on the whole, regard it their duty to serve their masters all the time, and in the midst of the running about and drudgery, they manage to eat what they get.

The case with the bondmen in respect of God, on the contrary, is that their primary occupation is with their own affairs and interests, and observe the duty to God only in what little time they can spare from worldly activities. They, for instance, offer Namaz or donate money for a noble cause and believe they have done all that needed doing by way of fulfilling the obligations to the Lord and the Faith. The claim of bondage, in fact, is that real and regular occupation should be with things appertaining to Faith while eating, drinking and earning of livelihood etc., received a secondary place. It does not, at all, mean that people abandoned their business or profession, but only this much that whatever was done was subordinate to loyalty to God."

x) The Maulana said: "The principal aim and purpose. of our endeavour is to teach the Muslims all the things the holy Prophet had brought with him, i.e., to integrate the Ummat with the whole of the practical and conceptual structure of Islam. This is our primary object. As for the setting out of *Jama'ats* and *Tabligh* rounds, these are the elementary means to the realisation of that end, while the teaching of the Kalima and Namaz are, so to speak, the ABC of our curriculum."

xi) The Maulana said: "Our *Tabligh* workers must not feel disheartened if their call falls on deaf ears at some place and they are cursed, and false charges are levelled against them. On such occasions, they should remind themselves that this is the special Summat and legacy of the Prophets. To be humiliated in the path of God is not everyone's good fortune. And when they are received with warmth and dignity and their call is heeded to, they should regard it wholly a favour of the Lord and feel grateful to Him for it. The service and education of the seekers, however lowly they may be, must always be considered an act of giving thanks on this favour. The Quranic verse, *He frowned and turned away because the blind man came to him* (LXXX: 1-2), imparts the same lesson. They should, further, be watchful against the deception of the self and avoid the folly of regarding success and popularity to be their own achievement. There is, also, a great danger of 'saint-worship' in it which must, further, be guarded against."

xii) The Maulana said: "Make it clear to all the workers that while they should not pray to God for hardship in this path (one should always pray for peace and safety), if the Lord sends down a trouble or affliction, they should consider it a blessing from Him, and an atonement for their sins, and a source of elevation in ranks. Such calamities in the way of God are the food and drink of the Apostles, the devout, and the truthful."

xiii) The Maulana said: "A very wrong trend that has set in is that if the others accept the things we say, we consider it to be our success and if they reject them, we consider it to be our failure, though it is wholly incorrect to think like that in this path. To accept or reject is the act of others, so, why should we be deemed successful or otherwise for what the others do. Our success lies only in this much that we did our best. If the others do not agree, it is their failure. How can we be regarded unsuccessful on account of their refusal? People have forgotten. They have come to believe that to cause anyone to accept, which, in fact, is the work of God, is their own responsibility, though their duty lies only in striving in the right way. It was not demanded even of the Apostles to cause anyone to accept anything.

"What we should learn from our failure is that, perhaps, there was some fault or deficiency in our endeavour; we had not been able to discharge our duty properly, and that was why, God had shown us that result. After it, we should resolve to multiply our efforts and intensify our quantitatively." supplications, both qualitatively and

xiv) The Maulana said: "Time is a running train of which hours, minutes and seconds are, as one would say, the compartments, and our activities and occupations are the passengers sitting in them. Now, our worthless worldly affairs have occupied the train of our life so completely that they do not allow the good and noble deeds that are related to the Hereafter to get in. Our task, therefore, lies in acting resolutely and making the deeds that are likely to earn for us the good pleasure of the Lord and lead to felicity in After-life take the place of the valueless affairs and interests of this world."

xv) The Maulana said: "However good a deed we may perform, it should be brought to an end with Istighfar, i.e., earnest repentance. Repentance should form the concluding part of every act of ours. Sincere regrets should be expressed, and forgiveness begged of the Lord believing that there must have remained some deficiency in the carrying out of it. The sacred Prophet ended every Namaz with Istighfar, and, so, also, should every act of a preacher end on it. The bondsman can never perform an act of God as is His due."

xvi) One day when after Fajr prayers a large number of *Tabligh* workers were present and the Maulana was feeling so weak that he could not address them even from the bed, he had the following message communicated to them through an attendant:

"All your *Tabligh* activities will be to no avail if, along with them, you do not pay proper attention to *Ilm* (Learning) and *Zikr* (God-remembrance). Ilm and *Zikr* are the two wings without which one cannot fly in these surroundings. What is more, if *Ilm* and *Zikr* are neglected, this endeavour may become a new source of mischief. Without *Ilm*, Islam and Iman are a mere formality, and without *Zikr*, Ilm is pure darkness. Effulgence is produced in Ilm by *Zikr*, and the real fruits of *Zikr* are gained only when *Ilm*, too, is there. The Devil often makes the ignorant Sufis his tools. The importance of Ilm and Zikr should, therefore, not be overlooked in this regard otherwise, the *Tabligh* endeavour will end up in waywardness, and, God forbid, you will be in great loss."

(What it shows is that *Tabligh* workers should not consider the tours etc., to be the whole thing, as the case, generally, is today, but, also, regard the study and teaching of Faith and remembrance of God and the forging of a living bond with Him a most important duty. In other words, they are not only to be 'soldiers' and preachers, but students of Faith and truthful bondmen of the Lord as well).

xvii) The Maulana said: "It is necessary for people taking part in the *Tabligh* work to believe whole-heartedly in the reward promised and the glad tidings given, in the Quran and the Traditions, on striving in the path of Faith through preaching and propagation. They should join in the *Tabligh* endeavour solely in the hope and desire of winning those rewards and favours. They must, further, tell themselves that God will, according to His promise, grant them, also, the reward equal in value to the entire reward that will be earned, through their deeds, by men who will be led to goodness through their worthless efforts as well as by those who will take to Faith, till the Doomsday, as a result of this endeavour provided their intention is sound and exertions worthy of acceptance."

xviii) The Maulana said: "The main end and purpose of religious efforts should be the seeking of the countenance of the Lord and the earning of the recompense of the Hereafter. As for the favours promised in this world, for example, a life a peace and honour or power and rule on the earth, these are the promised and not the desired ends. Or, in other words, all that we do should be with the object of earning the good pleasure of God and the reward of the Hereafter, and at the same time, also, believe in the things promised-and even pray for them, but we must not make them the aim and object of our worship etc., You will, perhaps, be able to understand the difference between the 'desired' and the 'promised' better with the help of the example that while the aim of marriage is to get a wife and derive satisfaction from her, dowry, also, comes with her which, so to speak, is indirectly 'promised.' Yet there is hardly a fool in the world who will marry solely for dowry- and suppose anyone does so and the wife comes to know that he has not married her but the dowry, what place will he have in her heart?"

xix) The Maulana said: "*The best Zikr of every occasion is to give heed to the commandment prescribed for it. O ye who believe!*

Let not your wealth and your children distract you from remembrance of Allah. (LXIII:9). Thus, whoever observes the God gives laws in his behaviour towards his children and in other worldly affairs life buying and selling, carries out the Zikr of Allah even while engaged in the."

xx) The Maulana said: "Persuade the people to go out of their homes, at their own expense, for the sake of learning and teaching of Faith and for spreading it. In case they are not in a position to bear the expenses or are not willing to make the sacrifice, arrange for the money from their own neighbourhood, and if even that is not possible then from some other place. Care should, however, be taken that the habit of Ishraaf-i-Nafs[1] does not develop in them which is highly destructive to Faith.

"It should, further, be made clear to those who set out in the path of God that hardships and hunger and thirst they may have to bear must be treated as a blessing from Above. These trials and difficulties are, indeed, the food of the Apostles and the sincerely devoted bondsmen of God."

xxi) The Maulana said: "The workers of our *Tabligh* movement should go to three classes of men. with three different aims. To the Ulema and the godly men they should go with the object of acquiring the knowledge of Faith and benefiting from their company to those of who are of a lower grade than themselves, for attaining perfection in Faith through the dissemination of religious light and

---

[1] Meaning the inclination to look up to the bondmen instead of the Lord for help in one's needs.

learning, and to the rest, for absorbing the various virtues that may be found in them."

xxii) The Maulana said: "Utmost effort ought to be made to associate men of religion, i.e., the Ulema and the pious and virtuous persons with the *Tabligh* movement and to allay their doubts and misgivings, and where it may be found that they are still unconvinced and in disagreement with us, a good interpretation should be put on their opposition, and their company should be sought with the object of learning from them and partaking of their blessings."

xxiii) The Maulana said: "I believe that the real ailment of the Muslims, at present, is that their hearts are devoid of religious consciousness and no eagerness is found in them for, seeking the knowledge of Faith. If religious inclination and appreciation of the importance of the Faith is produced in their hearts, Islamism will be revived in them in no time. This, for the present, is the real aim of our endeavours and not merely the teaching or correction of the Kalima etc."

xxiv) The Maulana said: "In our programme, setting out in the path of Faith, in the form of *Jama'ats*, occupies the foremost place. The chief advantage of it is that a man comes out of the traditional into a healthy and dynamic environment in which there is a great scope for the development of his religious sentiments. Moreover, the Mercy of the Lord is drawn towards him, in particular, on account of the hardships he has to undergo in travelling from place to place for the preaching and propagation of Faith."

xxv) The Maulana said: "When I call in a physician, I have the *Tabligh* mission in my mind, and I aim at using the occasion to make him interested in the work of God. That is why, I allow only those physicians to be brought of my treatment about whom there is some hope that they can be useful for the religious endeavour."

xxvi) The Maulana said: "An important principle of our Movement is that while in a public speech the accent ought to be on severity, in informal conversation, greatest leniency should be on severity, in informal conversation, greatest leniency should be shown. As far as possible, a general talk should be preferred for the reform of the people so much so that if a wrong or undesirable thing is seen in a close friends or colleague, it should be sought to be corrected through a public address. This, also, was the method of the sacred Prophet. Even when he had to admonish people who were close to him, he used to speak in general terms, such as, 'The state of some people is that Should it seem necessary to speak individually, apart from adopting a mild and affectionate attitude, care should, also, be taken not to reprove straightaway, as, in such a case, it often happens that the ego of a person is aroused and he begins to defends himself and enters into an argument. Hence, it should be overlooked at that time, and he should be warned on some other and more appropriate occasion."

xxvii) The Maulana said: "Those who are engaged in the *Tabligh* work should have contacts with people belonging to all classes and levels. These should include the Ulema, the men who remember God much, the English-educated persons, the traders and the common people. It will be most helpful in understanding the nature and functioning of our mission and in directing and regulating its affairs and, also, provide the foundation for the promotion of unity and co-operation among the different sections of Muslims which is our aim."

xxviii) The Maulana said: "In a religious endeavour the portion of the sincere and truthful ones is only the attainment of the good pleasure of the Lord and the Prophet, and when gifts and worldly goods come to hand, the claim of the weak and the indigent persons and of those whose hearts are to be reconciled should receive primary attention. It is for this reason that I say that when people who have not yet realised the significance of our mission and do not feel drawn towards it are called, the fare should be paid to them and they should be treated with utmost kindness while no such trouble need be taken in respect of the sincere ones who appreciate the reality of our endeavour and have already associated themselves with it."

xxix) The Maulana said: "If some poor persons are willing to accompany a *Tabligh Jama'at* on a tour but they are hard pressed for money, effort should made, as far as possible, to persuade a few rich people of the same place to go along with them and it should be explained what a vast reward there is on helping the poor and indigent brothers who set out in the path of Faith. At the same time, they should, also, be told that if they want to help a poor colleague, they must enquire about the rules and principles of it from the more experienced workers and act only on their advice. Helping anyone the wrong way and without regard to the principles often does more harm than good."

The Maulana, then, laid down a few guidelines, and, as far as I remember, also, told us to note them down. These were:

(a) The poor should be helped in such a way that they did not start looking forward to it as a matter of course and fell a prey to Ishraaf-i-Nafs.

(b) The giving should only be for Talif, i.e., for producing an inclination for Faith. It should, thus, only be as much as was required, and, then, reduced gradually as solicitude for Faith and devotion to the *Tabligh* work may increase, and through friendly talk and good counsel the urge ought to be created in them to strive earnestly and meet the expenses themselves, and thinking it to be a most important need, even borrow for i, if the occasion demands, in the same way as they borrow for the worldly needs. To avoid being under anyone's obligation in this path is a mark of deep heartedness. At the time of Migration, Hazrat Abu Bakr had offered a camel to the sacred Prophet, but the Prophet had preferred to settle its price and then, buy it on trust.

But as long as the eagerness and inclination is not created, necessary monetary help should be extended to the needy co-workers.

(c) It is necessary for monetary help to be given secretly arid with sentiments of regard and respect and the givers should feel grateful to the recipients who were engaged in religious work for accepting it and consider them superior to themselves for, in spite of poverty, they had left their homes and undertaken the journey for the sake of the Faith. To set out in the service of Islam is among the attributes of *Hijrat*[1], and to help those who do so is among the attributes of *Nusrat*[2], and the *Ansar*[3] can never be on a par with *Muhajir*[4].

(d) Help should, generally, be given to *Tabligh* workers in the form of *Hadiya* (Gift) and not *Zakat* (Poor-due) or *Sadqa* (Charity). *Zakat* and Sadqa are like the bubbly foam or waste material of a pot which must be taken out otherwise the whole dish would be spoilt while Hadiya is like adding perfume to a dish or applying a gold or silver leaf to it.

(e) A very good way of showing concern for those who set out of their homes for the sake of Faith and helping them is to visit their families, enquire after their welfare and perform such chores as bringing the daily provisions from the market. They should tell them how fortunate their male members were to have gone out on such a magnificent mission.

(f) To keep oneself informed privately of the circumstances of those who are serving the cause of Faith-what were their needs and how were they spending their days?

An excellent form of it can be that well-to-do persons sent the ladies of their households to the families of the *Tabligh* workers who went out on tours. It will lend encouragement to the family

---

[1] The reference is to the Migration of the early Muslims from Mecca to Medina.

[2] Meaning the aid and support extended to the Muslim emigrants by the inhabitants of Mecca.

[3] The inhabitants of Medina who extended every help to the holy Prophet. and other Muslims on their migration to it.

[4] The Muslims who had migrated to Medina from Mecca and taken up residence there.

members of these workers as well as provide an opportunity to gain first-hand knowledge of their difficulties.

xxx) The Maulana said: "Without a shadow of doubt, the promises made by God are firm and positive while what a man thinks or plans on the basis of his knowledge or experience is speculative and conjectural. Yet, the position, today, is that people do not try as hard to prove worthy of the promises of the Lord by fulfilling the essential conditions as they do for the realisation of their own aims and ambitions. It shows that they have more faith in their imaginary calculations than in God's promises. This is not confined to the common people, but everyone, from the highest to the lowest, is dyed in the same hue. The main object of our endeavour, thus, is to rid the Muslims of this malaise, and direct their lives and activities along the path of reliance upon the premises of the Lord. This is the way of the Divine Apostles, and this is what they have taught their followers, i.e., to make themselves deserving of the promises of God by putting their trust in them and striving sincerely to fulfil the attending conditions. God will treat you in accordance with your faith in His promises."

xxxi) The Maulana said: "Faith is not static. One either moves forward in it or falls back. It is like a garden. When a garden gets water and the weather, also, is favourable, it flourishes day by day, and when the weather becomes unfavourable and it is, also, not supplied with water, it starts withering. The same is true of man's faith."

xxxii) The Maulana said: "Think out ways of bringing the people to Faith and making them genuinely interested in its service (in the same way as the worldly-minded persons are always thinking of the ways of promoting their interests), and approach everyone in the manner that may be most effective with him."

xxxiii) The Maulana said: "By nature, man is more. susceptible to despondency because it helps him to feel that he is not responsible for his actions and there is nothing be can do. Know well that it is a great deception of the Devil and of your own self."

xxxiv) The Maulana said: "To lose heart owing to lack of resources shows that your reliance is upon material means and you have little faith in the promises of God and in His Unseen Powers. The Lord provides the means when one rises up with faith in Him and a stout heart, otherwise what can a man do by himself. But it is essential to have courage and strive to the best of one's ability."

xxxv) The Maulana said: "In our view, the process of correction and reform should follow this order: (After the renewal of the covenant with God through the *Kalima*), primary attention ought to be paid to the correction and perfection. of Namaz. The propitiousness of Namaz will reform the whole life. The correction of Namaz is the source of the correction of whole life, and it is through the reform and perfection of Namaz. that the rest of the life is blessed with virtue and perfection."

xxxvi) The Maulana said: "Generally, workers run after big and influential persons and do not pay much attention to the poor people even if they come to them voluntarily. This is materialism. Know well that whoever comes to you voluntarily is a gift of God and whoever is brought by persuasion is your own acquisition, and a gift from the Lord is, naturally, more valuable than one's own earnings. Hence, pay fullest attention to the poor, indigent Mewatis that are staying here and remember that the holy Prophet had made this prayer for himself: O God! Keep me alive in the state of indigence, and grant me death in the state of indigence, and raise me up, on the Day of Resurrection, in the company of the indigent."

xxxvii) The Maulana said: "Co-operation and mutual consultation is most essential for our work. Without it, there is a great danger."

xxxviii) The Maulana said: "Whoever takes part in the *Tabligh* movement should devote himself particularly to *Ilm* (Learning) and *Zikr* (God- remembrance) when he goes on a tour. Religious advancement is not possible without Ilm and *Zikr*. It should, further, be done with attachment to the elders and under their guidance.

"The *Ilm* and *Zikr* of the Apostles was under the guidance of God and that of the blessed Companions, under the guidance of the holy Prophet. After the passing away of the sacred Prophet, men of Ilm and Zikr are, so to speak, his deputies for everyone. Hence, in Ilm and Zikr we cannot do without the guidance of the elders.

"Moreover, during a *Tabligh* tour, a person must concentrate wholly on his special duties, to the exclusion of all other activities and interests. The special duties are: *Tabligh* rounds, *Ilm* and *Zikr*, service of the companions in the journey, in particular, and mankind, in general, correction of intention and cultivation of the habits of sincerity and Ihtisab."

xxxix) The Maulana said: "Alas! Faith in the promises of God has died away. Recreate it and learn to make it the basis of all your acts. Further, do not interpret the assurance on your own for your knowledge is most limited. The meaning you draw from the promises of the Lord must be in keeping with His glory, and you ought to beseech Him to fulfil His promises in the manner that may be worthy of His Might and Magnificence. How can you form a correct idea of the reality of the boons of the Hereafter when a celestial Tradition declares that 'the boons and favours God has got ready for His truthful Believers in Heaven are such that no eye has seen or ear heard of them, nor has an idea of these blessings ever crossed the human mind.'

"We have done a great harm to ourselves by imagining about the Divine promises on the strength of our own understanding and experience and basing our hopes and expectations upon it. The munificence of the Lord will be worthy of His glory."

xi) The Maulana said: "Faith requires that what is pleasing to God and the Apostle should, also, be pleasing to the bondsman, and what is hateful to God and the Apostle should, also, be hateful to him. Hurt is caused by the needle in the same way as it is by the sword. God and the Apostle, thus, feel sad and annoyed at Apostasy and Polytheism as well as at evildoing. We, too, should have a feeling of pain and aversion for evildoing."

xii) The Maulana said: "Mosques are the daughters of Masjid-i-Nabwi[1] and, therefore, all the things that were done in Masjid-i-Nabwi should, also, be done in them. In addition to the celebration

---

[1] Meaning the Prophet's Mosque in Medina.

of Namaz, training and instruction was, also, imparted in Masjid-i-Nabwi, and all other affairs appertaining to the preservation and propagation of the Faith, such as, the despatch of preaching parties and even the organisation of military campaigns were carried out in it. What I want is that all these things should be done, in the same way. In our mosque as well."

(xiii) The Maulana said: "My position should not be deemed to be higher than that of an ordinary Believer. It is irreligiousness to do something simply because I say it. Examine whatever I say in the light of the Quran and the Sunnah, and think over it yourself, and then, act on your own responsibility. I can only advise. As Hazrat Omar used to say to the Companions: 'You have placed a heavy responsibility on my shoulders. Now, all of you must keep a watch on what I do.' I request my friends to observe my actions vigilantly and check me when I go wrong, and, also to pray for my guidance along the right path."

www.ingramcontent.com/pod-product-compliance
Ingram Content Group UK Ltd.
Pitfield, Milton Keynes, MK11 3LW, UK
UKHW021406190726
13845UKWH00028B/904

9 789394 770331